FOSSIL REMAINS OF MYTHICAL CREATURES

BY BOB SLAUGHTER

SMILODONESS BOOKS

DALLAS, TEXAS

I wish dedicate this book to the ladies who encouraged and helped me through a life of adventure; Billie Mae Vernon, Juliana Bernier, Nell Westberry, Diana, Ellen, and Marie.

I am indebted to George Toomer, Dave Thomas, who read the manuscript and offered many suggestions, and to his son, Dave Thomas Jr., who prepared the locality maps from field notes.

Erick Espinoza and Lucy Stiffler were indispensable in the actual publication of the book. The photography was done by Juliana Bernier, Wendell Dickason, and Mike McKool. Thanks are also due to those fellow adventurers who made so many of the "discoveries" outlined in this volume.

CONTENTS

Illustrations

Introduction

Until man solved his identity crisis by creating gods in his own image, he was a snivling little wretch— certainly not the master species he uses for a mirror. He doesn't have the enduring power of roaches. He can't survive unaided in the wilds (he can't even win a battle with the mosquito or fly), and he doesn't have the sense of a rodent, who will hole up in shelter during the hot summer day, rainstorm or freeze. And, unlike the other creatures, from the giant whale to the pollywog, he depends on myth for information, inspiration, and explanation of his existence. "What you don't know wont hurt you" thinking prevails as a path of least resistance for those who lack self motivation, or seek an eternal Big Daddy who will furnish tidbits when one is in a jam. A people's mythology remains as a loose putty stuck and smeared between stones that don't fit, or have no business being placed together, in order to support a continually crumbling foundation, which we build our shaky civilazations atop. Superstition, the relgious thought of the moment, becomes "mythology" and insignificant thinking only in the shadow of the new, popular myth supported by a civilization, also replacing the old— Babylonian myth fell to Hebrew myth, Greek myth fell to Roman myth, which fell to Christian myth, and so on. One dare not say that the prevailing power of superstition is mythology—to imply that a prevailing superstition (religion) is as much mythology as its predecessor is to invite certain wrath and retribution. To suggest that land smoting by Zeus, the supreme Greek sky and weather god, is no more mythological than Yahweh's great flood smote, or God's current smiting of drug addicts and homosexuals with HIV virus, is folly when

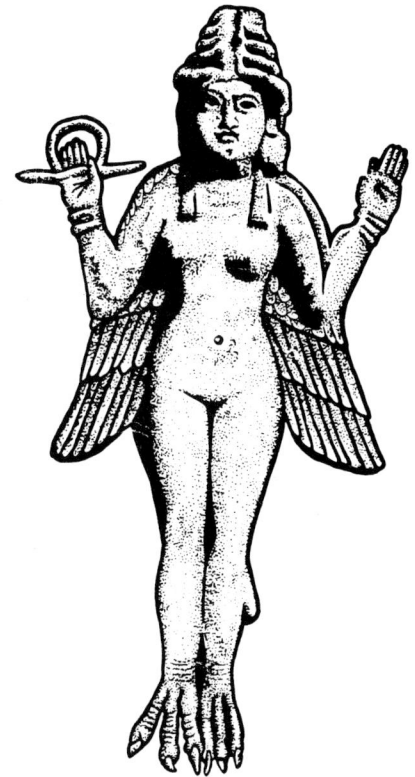

addressing one steeped in popular myth...a believer. The question needing address at this point is whether one can pick and choose one's myth. Can you buy an Arch Angel myth or Jonah's whale while rejecting mermaids, fairies, and unicorns? I think not. To open the door of myth and the mystical side one finds there is no sign reading "You must be this high to get on this ride." There is no template for size and shape...The Aboriginal Bunyip, the Japanese Oni, the flute playing Pan, and Moses are pretty much of similar size. If one mythological example is accepted then it becomes hypocritical to disregard another...can we laugh at Santa Claus, the Easter Bunny and the Tooth Fairy while placing a call for an exorcist to chase away a demonic posession (why does the devil never possess the home of a MIT professor?). A true believer of one mythical standard can't in good conscience, poo-poo the standard of another— again, if one is to totally accept the spirituality and veracity of one's own set of mythical rules, heroes and legends, the seperation of myth and reality become a moot point. By stipulating the existance of one spiritual, ethereal, or mystic, form the world is immediately divided into at least two planes: the worldly plane on which we drive through 5:00 o'clock traffic with a short stop for milk at the 7-ll, and the mystical plain of the supernatural, where devils, ghosts, fairies, Voo Doo dolls, blessed candles, chicken gut reading, fortune telling and perfect Bingo cards exist. Suddenly we must accept Shiva, Buddha, Aztec gods, and possibly the fact that Elvis, James Dean, and Bruce Lee might well be alive. The concept of Pantheism becomes an issue as we aren't sure whether the world's other gods might be a little tougher than our own—our little devil , though not much of a force among some of the mud gods on Pacific islands, gives our god a fit. Maybe a Pacific devil would be a tough cookie indeed...certainly no other god, good or bad, should be ignored—just in case they hang around the hereafter, as well.   Now we look to the second level of mystery: mythical creatures and people. Are they real? Did they exist in another time? If we accept myth as reality, we can't really say for sure. If we allow a burning bush to speak, or loaves of bread to multiply, it only seems fair that we allow Leprechauns to multiply gold coins. If angels can fit on pinheads and fly about, then the logical step invites the flying demon, Isusu, on his flights around Beirut—where a lot of people have seen a lot of things flying around for thousands of years. I would never be so bold as to accept one over the other—a flying mystery is a flying mystery, well beyond the understanding of mere mortals. Something flew over my yard, leaving a strong current of air in the smoke of my brisket. It could have been Isusu, a vampire, a winged monster or a protecting angel...I'll pick the angel because the other three are too scary for me to think about. It might affect my next attempt to grill out in the open, and I'm planning to try trout which is pretty delicate anyway - its also expensive and I don't think one of God's angels would mess with it, while Isusu could queer the deal!

Bob Slaughter knows his business when it comes to fossil remains. As a Professor of Paleontology, he has spent a lifetime digging for facts to support known theories and thesis. He has proven when certain rodents moved from one land mass to another for instance. While there have always been the skeptical Flat Earth people, his audience was that of the educated, who needed proof to support an already good guess. Its only natural that he need to search for truth would lead him toward a much harder arena. "Mystical creatures and extinct creatures actually have a lot in common,"says Slaughter. "The extinct creatures have bones but no

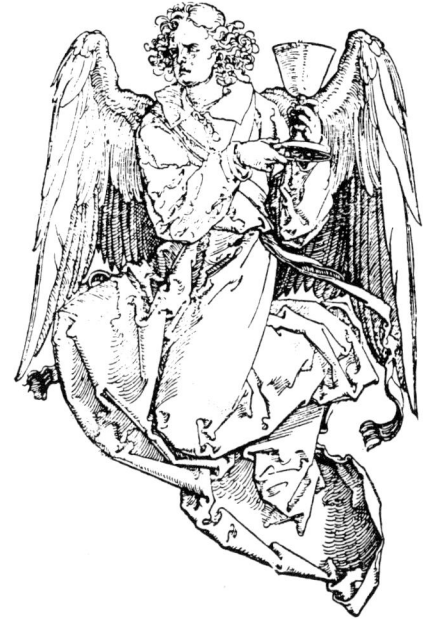

dialogue...Mythical creatures have dialogue that cultures have created for them but they have no other reality...I think the myths are the true story anyway..." Returning to my own thesis, man has put words and stories into potentially mythical gods much the same as he has put his own spin on mythical creatures... Don't be getting out of bed and hanging around mother and daddy's bedroom door, or the Boogie Man (Isusu, flying monster, werewolf, or devil) will get you!" Actually, I think that many boogie men were used primarily to keep teenagers out of the woods at night—every male god loves a virgin.

Are the creatures we see here real? If Professor Slaughter had found the original Voo Doo doll, would the believers of that faith answer in the negative? If he had found Jesus' sandal, the stone tablets of the Ten Commandments, or nails of the cross, our acceptance would depend on our faith ...they could be real! Could they be of manufacture by believers long since dead? We must remember the souvenir salesmen of the crusades who sold pieces of the cross and the bones of the apostles by the thousands—they were real to the buyer who placed fingerbones in alters across Europe as a matter of faith. If Prof.Slaughter said they came in a revelation and were "revealed" to him, what person who accepts mythology, spirits and devils could argue that their creation wasn't guided by the mystical world—something like equivalent of "the gift of tongues" which is readily accepted if spoken by one with fantastic hair and a bad fashion sense. Perhaps Professor Slaughter has been given the gift of creativity seen through a mystical eye. Having worked in many countries of mystery, could there be a chance that one of their gods saw fit to intervene with revelation—possibly the mythical creature was a particular god's pride and joy, while it may not worked out for the best, the god wanted a little credit for originality. In the Pantheist spirit, we might think of something like a Pantheist Universal Mystery Craft Show where each god submits his best shot like a divine use of pipecleaners. Since gods are often limited in their work by remaining unseen to human eyes, the possibility of choosing one mortal as a creative pipeline isn't so far fetched...it happens nightly on religious channels across the world, and in the mud and grass huts where witch doctors read animal guts. The daring of Slaughter's work, with its potential for ridicule among skeptics, is akin to handling of vipers and the drinking of poisonous liquids among certain faithful souls—maybe more because the snake and the poison shows are performed in front of those who find such mysteries common place, while the fossils of mythical creatures are presented to a biased public. The question of authenticity is no more important than that of religious relics. Does viewing them give one a sense of calm, an answer to mysterious questions: a final rest for disturbance, "So that's what a mermaid skeleton looks like?" I always wondered. Now I can get on with my daily life without pondering such things beyond my ability." In this sense Slaughter has performed a miraculous service as he has closed a frustrating gap in history...whether the ancient superstitions and mythical pheonmenon or more importantly, modern superstitions? Thanks to Professor Slaughter we need not have an answer. Just knowing that somebody has taken a stand lets us off the hook. Realizing that a person has gone through a great deal of training and effort that we would never have attempted, makes him an authority on such things. We simply don't have to think! He, like the Pope, takes full responsability so we can watch the Superbowl without interruption of haunting thoughts. Slaughter doesn't say they are real. He simply says "They exist...they are." How Zen: how cosmic; how mystical!" We are not asked to make a profound judgment, other than will they look good on a coffee table? If only other mystical questions were so easy. There is really no right or wrong answer when dealing with the mystical—one accepts or rejects according to one's current popular faith in such things. There are thousands of answers; we have but to pick one and stick with it until a better one comes along. All shall be revealed on our passing when we take our myths to the grave. Maybe we've created such a fine myth that it will live on after we are dust...like Buffalo Bill, George Washington's cherry tree caper or the kids who saw Our Lady of Lourdes - what if Bob discovered her handbag?   Real or fiction? Who cares? Owning a myth of a myth is just as valid as owning reality of a myth which would destroy mythical joy...how sad to find that there really is an old fat guy at the north pole who stops giving people nice presents when they reach the age of six—a poor fellow who never gets to see the expression on kid's faces or who will never be able to go and buy a Big Mac. I personally will settle for a bite taken out of a cookie and a half consumed glass of milk as proof of Santa's existance. I will sit and enjoy the skeletal remains of Tiki or the armor of Neptunoides without questioning. I have faith. As I listen to the attacks and ranting of the unfaithful, it will only make me stronger. I will dwell in the house of belief as I consider the fact that there is nothing so passionate as vested interest disguised as intellectual or moral conviction...those who berate my belief are those who stand to profit the most from its demise. If I pay to own the remains of Kokopelli in a stuccoed burial basket rather than a "blessed" aerosol spray, a model of St.Christopher magnetized for my car dash, Tammy Faye's eyeliner, Oral Robert's ballpoint pen that has hands rising to the top of his prayer tower in liquid or

Robert Tilton's "Miracle Anointed Oil" (which happens to be nothing but a sealed handy wipe) who loses? Not me! I knew the truth going in...the "truth" is whatever I want it to be. A perfect faith...a real mystery resolved at my whim. Instant happyness.   A hoax is when someone is fooled. It's different from a lie in my opinion. Generally, only a fool can be a victim of a hoax, while the victim of a lie is usually one who had the faith to believe and was misled. Since we are dealing with myth, there is already no impliication of absolute truth, therefore there can be no hoax or lie unless self imposed—this is the major difference between Slaughter's creatures and man's superstition and prevailing myths. We can visit his exhibits with little fear of being killed by a fanatic wrapped in dynamite in support of his myth ,whose toes have been stepped upon. If relics of popular myths be presented as Professor Slaughter has done, the world might gain insight into its folly and we could move beyond our wooden headresses to assume responsability for our actions, past and present. We could forgive the flying monsters their terror, the mean tricks of El Nahual, the witch burnings, and the Inquisition as we realize that "Man" is just a "Guy", a silly fellow looking for a little extra help from Neptune, mermaids, and fairies—a pot of gold hidden by a tiny man in green or the answer to a prayer to quell fear and suffering. Its only human to believe.

George Toomer
Eliade Professor of
Comparative Religion
Ladonia University

ABOUT THE AUTHOR

During the twenty five years Bob Slaughter was Professor of Paleontology and Director of the Shuler Museum, he published three books and over one hundred articles and scholarly papers.

He was President of the Texas Academy of Science in 1971-72 and received the *Award for Outstanding Contributions to Earth Science* from the American Federation of Mineralogical Societies in 1983. Slaughter was also one of twelve American Professors cited by People Magazine for teaching excellence.

Prof. Slaughter has lectured on more than fifty American campuses, as well as in England, Spain, Lebanon, Egypt, Panama, Mexico and Canada. His expeditions to Europe the Middle East and Latin America were sponsored by the National Geographic Society, Smithsonian Institution, National Science Foundation and the Institute for the Study of Earth and Man at Southern Methodist University where he is now Professor Emeritus.

PROLOGUE

From 1965 to 1985, I spent a lot of time in the western Egyptian Desert between the Nile Valley and Libya, particularly in the Qattara Depression. This is an area some 75 by 150 miles deflated to 450 feet below sea level and is as near total desert as one can get. While prospecting for fossil bones there, one often is separated from one's colleagues by a mile or so— at least out of eye and ear shot— and one feels not only separated from our species, but from life in general. At such times, our insignificance is felt acutely. I've had similar feelings when deep in caves and on the open sea. It tends to make one more philosophical than usual.

At such times, I am often saddened by how little we know about the magnificent animals we are seeking; wonderful antelope with five horns, beavers the size of bears, shrews with live body weight less than a dime, horses the size of collie dogs, all singing their hearts out and putting their all into their mating dances for millions of years, and there was no one to see and appreciate them. Did the tiny horses whinny, or bray?

One time, while standing in the shade of a boulder taking a break, the extinct animals were parading for me in the bleak valley where they once roamed when suddenly it dawned on me that extinct animals and mythical creatures have something in common. Neither is complete, and each has what the other needs for completion. We don't know the color of the extinct forms, the noises they made, and we know almost nothing of their behavior. Because of their fossil record we do know something of their history, such as where they originated, evolved and migrated to and from.

Mythical creatures have been with man since his mind began to wander from his next meal and we know what kind of tools and weapons they had, what they wore, if anything, and even in some cases, a bit of their dialogue. However, the mythical creature lacks the kind of reality that comes with a fossil history.

I'm very proud of the light I've been able to reflect on the lives of extinct animals, their climatic tolerances and preferences, their geographic ranges, etc., but I'm getting a little old for extended expeditions, so perhaps I can do something for the mythical creatures, I thought. From the beginning I felt a sort of invisable influence guiding me, aiding me, reccommending to me. It was as if the mythical creatures were presenting themselves to me, one at a time, in actuality.

I have deepest respect for human cultures, both past and present, both highly developed and so-called archaic. I find it rather interesting that many of the legends outlive the culture that created them, some passed on by word of mouth and some through art and/or the written word. Usually these creatures were created and served to modify human behavior through religion. In fact, most of the mythical creatures owe their existence to religion. They invoked emotion through their "presence" in society, whether through fear, dreams of pleasure, or just plain humor.

All of us have conjured up images of fairies or gnomes while reading stories about them. Indeed, people still report encounters with leprechauns, demons and the like. As a paleontologist, I understand that evolution is not a theory, but a fact proven to me each time I excavate. Disbelievers' greatest misunderstanding is thinking that Darwin's

Theory is that "evolution happened." Evolution is as proven as gravity. Darwin's THEORY only involves the minutae of the mechanics by which it took place. Therefore as a paleontologist, it is extremely difficult to even imagine how a mermaid could come to pass. Fishes and mammals have been separated far too long for a simple cross to take place (mermaids). The same is true for goats and man (i.e., Pan). If I'm to ponder mythical creatures as real entities, for whatever reasons, I have to come to grip with this.

I am indebted to the Rod Serlings of the world for the idea of more than one plane of existence being inhabited in the same place and time. As speculative, and seemingly unprovable, as this idea is, it seems the only route to explain creatures that seem impossible combinations of animal forms. In another plane, different rules may be in effect and a mythical creature may have had a long evolution and a fairly complete fossil record, but being in another plane, we don't have access to it. Since they were/are known to our societies, they have the option of being figments of human imagination or crossing over occasionally, accounting for the myths themselves and the occasional modern sighting. If their time came while on one of these rare expeditions to our plane, that could be where their corpses remained. Unexpected death could occur via volcanic eruption, as may be the case of our example of the Japanese demon, Oni. It could come as an accident as in the case of theCliff End Fairies, or it might be a natural death which I perceive as coinciding with the end of the culture that believes in the creature (e.g., Kokopelli of the Anasazi). In any case, I now present you with some of the FOSSIL REMAINS OF MYTHICAL CREATURES which I hope, in death, will breath some life into these magnificent beings for you.

Verily,
Bob Slaughter

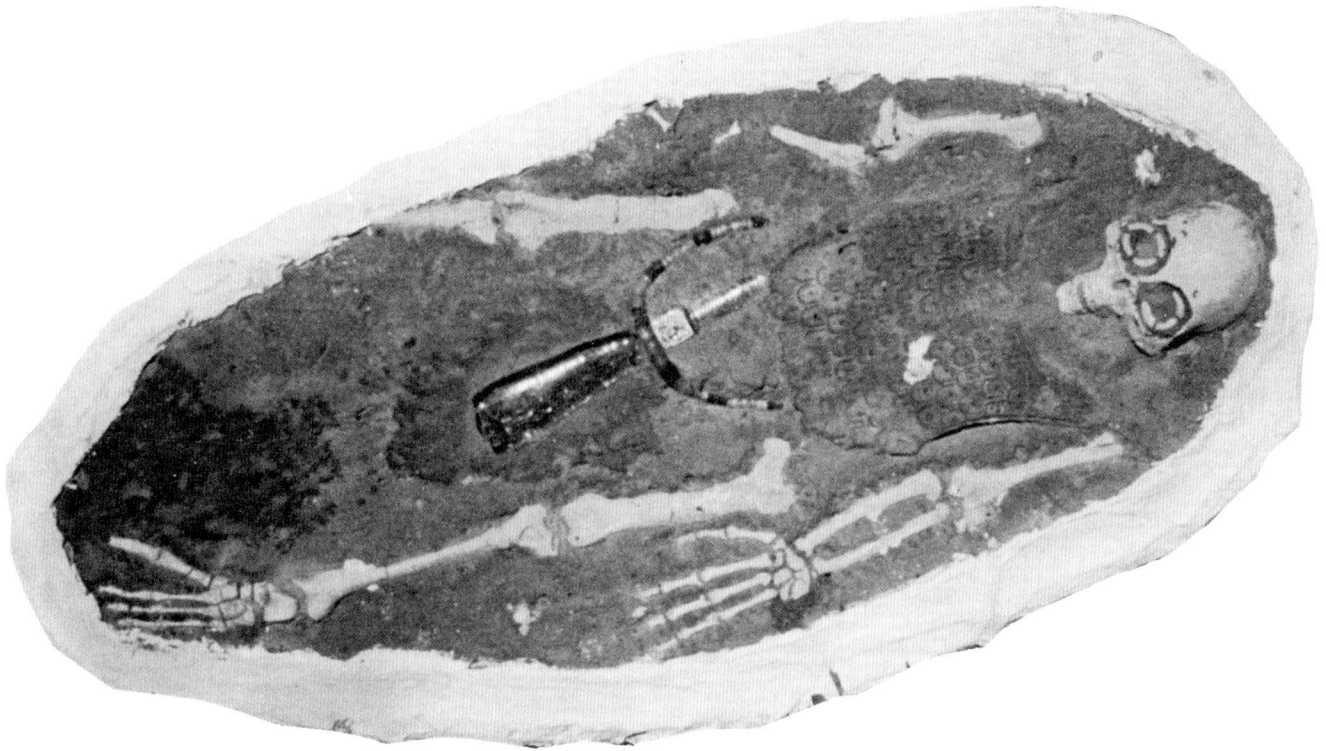

Figure 1 *Fossil of Alien skeleton.*

ALIEN

I am constantly amazed how some of the most important remains come to me. It is almost as if I was destined to speak for this array of strange creatures. For such a large percentage of all known fringe hominoids to have been discovered by myself and my friends defies probability. Now, for the only known remains of an extraterrestrial being to be discovered just four miles from our laboratories is surely is the most improbable of all.

The story of this discovery is in four distinct parts: (1) During the month of April 1897, numerous UFO sightings were reported from the Great Lakes to the Rio Grande, over a hundred in Texas alone. By far the most renowned is the described crash of a cigar shaped airship just outside the town of Aurora, Texas. According to S.E.Hayden, eye witness and author of an article that appeared in the Dallas Morning News (4/19/1897), early the morning of April 17, 1897, a cigar shaped airship flying low over Aurora, Texas, and traveling at only ten or twelve miles per hour, was viewed by a number of people. While amazed citizens watched, it crashed into a windmill on the property of Judge J. S. Proctor and exploded, fragmenting the pilot as well as the ship. The pilot's remains were buried the same day in the Aurora Cemetery. All that was said about the pilot was that it was a very small person, not of this world. Numerous pieces of a strange metal were collected shortly after the alleged crash,

near the destroyed windmill. To my knowledge however, no reliable metallurgical analyses have been reported, although it is said to be very unusual. (The grave was robbed in 1973 with the pilot's remains, metal placed in the grave and the tombstone all taken.)   (2) I make weekly ventures to the town of Ladonia, Texas where my wife, Juliana, was the Director of an Artist in Residence program. She, like many residents of Ladonia, is very interested in historical preservation. On one trip, we were having lunch at the Ladonia Emporium when she introduced me to Peter Betters. He had just purchased a turn-of-the-Century home on Main Street and was preparing to restore it. Juliana and I had looked at the grand old building and I was very pleased hear that it would be taken care of. I had discovered earlier the house had belonged Ethel McFarland, who was relative of a Dallas friend, Mike McFarland. Mike had told me that his "Old Maid" Aunt Ethel was quite beautiful, a fancy dresser and piano teacher, who lived alone all of her life. When I told Peter this, he countered that he had found letters in the old house indicating that for many years she had a secret gentleman friend, one Mr. Luther Mallow. I wasn't particularly interested in Aunt Ethel's love life but I became interested when he mentioned a letter referring to UFO observations he had made. Peter retrieved the letter, which was written in 1925, and we transcribed the part dealing with the airship.

"The night of April 16th, 1897, your family's lawyer, E. M. Roland, Colonel R. N. Burt and I were horseback. I was sort of a guide for a frog gigging expedition to the North Sulfur River north of town. Suddenly we saw some very bright lights

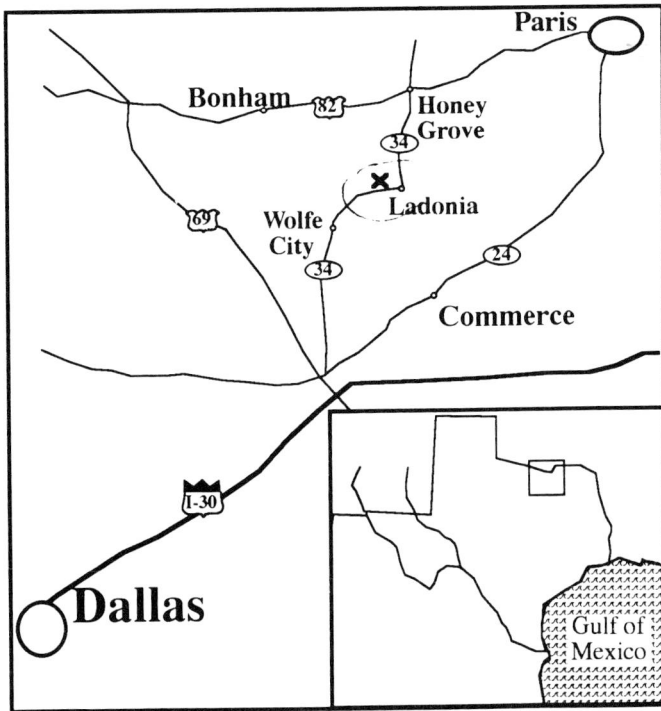

Figure 2 *Location of Alien discovery.*

on the floodplain some distance away. These lights were far brighter than any I had ever seen (you must remember that the only portable lights in that day were lanterns). We dismounted and approached on foot. When we were close enough, we lay between the cotton rows and observed several small "people" moving around two well lit cigar-shaped ships. Two of the "people" were going back and forth between the ships, while two others worked in the semidarkness at the edge of the light. We became frightened when the group stopped working and stared in our direction. When they began working again, we slipped away. The next day we met and returned to the site on horseback. Aside from the cotton being beaten down, all we found were two places side by side where the ground had been disturbed. It looked like two fresh graves. Rowland reported the incident that day, naming me and Burt as fellow witnesses. However, he was so ridiculed that Burt talked me into joining him in denying the event. Miffed, but unflinching, Roland changed the location of the sighting to his own property. I suspect to profit in some way or to save the graves for his personal exploitation, but he died shortly thereafter. I thought from time to time that I would excavate the graves myself, but after all these years I can't find the exact location."

It was early that next morning (April 17th) that the airship crashed in Aurora, Texas, less than a hundred miles to the west. It could have been one of the ships seen near Ladonia the night before. That afternoon (April 17th), C. L. McIlhaney, a farmer, reported sighting a cigar shaped airship on the ground near the Bosque River three miles from Stephenville, Texas. He fetched the mayor of Stephenville, the district attorney, two judges, two medical doctors, and a group of about fifty returned to the site. The group witnessed two small people scurrying about, apparently repairing the ship. This could have been the other ship seen near Ladonia the night before. (3) In 1929, the Corps of Engineers straightened the channel of the North Sulfur River, cutting off its meanders, to expedite runoff during flooding. One result was it initiated rapid downcutting and today the straightened channel is quite deep, exposing Cretaceous and Pleistocene deposits. These are very fossiliferous and attract numerous fossil hunters. As the only paleontologist around Ladonia, I often have fossil hunters stop by with bones for identification. (4) One day an avid collector, geologist Richard Wallace, brought me the distal end of a tibia (lower leg bone) that looked sort of like a human but was hollow, not unlike a bird bone. It was not fossilized and I thought it

3

might be a small deformed Indian, as there are many archeological sites buried in the floodplain. I asked Richard to show me exactly where he had found the bone and he took me to Davis Creek, a small, but deep, tributary that cuts across the floodplain on its way to the river just north of Ladonia (Fig.2). Sure enough, we found fragments of more "modern" bone eroding down the slope and about three feet from the surface was part of another long bone. Rather than tunnel into the bank, I decided to go topside and mark off a square and dig down, in case something would be found that needed to be documented. The burial was almost intact except for the right tibia Richard had found on the slope and most of the right ankle and foot bones disturbed by the creek's erosion. When the skull came into sight, I realized that there was a good chance this was the subject of Mr. Mallow's letter to Ethel McFarland. It matches very closely the faces we've all seen drawn after alleged encounters with extraterrestrial beings. The broncos is relatively large. The nasal opening is exceptionally small, as are the mouth and teeth. The eyes, on the other hand, are huge and in the sockets are sets of sclerotic rings, bony skeletons supporting the large eyeballs. Throughout the history of animals, very large eyeballs (some birds, fish, and dinosaurs) have developed these eye skeletons to help keep atmospheric, or water, pressure from collapsing them. All of the bones are hollow, except for the ribs, hand and foot bones, which are solid. This creature is clearly not human in the strict since, even though it can be considered hominoid.

Ladonia wallacia, new genus & species
Figure 1

Diagnosis: LU 63444. Large eyes with sclerotic rings, small mouth and nasals. Long bones very short for their transverse diameters and hollow. The long, attenuated hands have an opposed thumb and three equal length fingers, which like the thumb, have but a single finger joint—humans have two. The feet likewise have but four toes and the "big toe" is the longest and slightly opposed, perhaps reflecting arboreal ancestry.

Type locality: The east bank of Davis Creek, four miles north of Ladonia, Texas, 225 yards east of highway and 100 yards from the banks of the old Sulfur River channel (Fig. 2).

Etymology: *Ladonia* for the town where the remains were discovered + *wallacia* named for Richard Wallace, discoverer of the skeleton.

Discussion: The skeleton is wearing a sort of vest made of a material not unlike woven fibers of extruded glass. Also associated is a "belt" of metal "beads." The "beads" are a series of cradled "cups" of at least three types of metal. Considering the oxidation (patina), two are probably different copper alloys, and the other is something like aluminum. Also associated is a tongue-shaped piece of a glass. It is clear with a slight bluish tint. It is harder than most glass, but not particularly well produced for such a high-tech society. Attached is what could only be considered a handle which is made of a copper alloy and is gold plated. This object seems to be independent, and not a part of something else. Its use is unknown. It seems a poor choice of material for a bludgeon. The other possibilities that come to mind are a scepter, or other symbol of status; or a unit for communication (i.e.crystal for radio-communication).

By analogy, the relatively large brain may denote a high degree of intelligence. The large eyes doubtless denote an evolutionary need for vision in low light levels. The hollow bones could be interpreted as to lighten the body in a high gravity situation (i.e.large planet). I must admit, however, in the absence of any animals evolving in high gravity with which to compare, more sturdy bones

4

Figure 3 *Close up of Alien skull.*

might be more appropriate to handle the increased physical stress. Hollow bones could then suggest a low gravity habitat (i.e.small planet) with the limb bones having to deal with less physical stress. Whatever the case, these relatively fragile long bones would certainly be a disadvantage for a biped on Earth. Although right ulna-radius, wrist and hand bones are missing as well as right foot bones and the distal end of the right tibia, these are due to erosion of the burial site. No other bones are broken, in spite of their fragility, and there is no other evidence as to what caused its demise. The fact that there probably were two, plus the crash the following morning of one of the space ships at Aurora and the hasty repair of another near Stephenville suggest that the group was having some very serious problems.

5

J n 1970 while on my annual vacation to Port Aransas, Texas, I visited an old friend and former student, Walter Sohl. Walt is interested in everything and we started discussing the behavior of sand dunes. I have spent a lot of time in the Sahara Desert and he has considerable experience on the barrier islands of the Gulf and Atlantic coasts. He told me about a place where Hurricane Carla took out 250 yards of the Mustang Island's protective dunes back in 1961. As a result, the winds had deflated the surface down to a sort of hardpan. Hardpan sometimes develops when carbonates in the ground water percolate to the surface where the water evaporates. The carbonates then precipitate and cement the sand grains together, making sandstone.

We decided to drive down and have a look and I was fascinated. The area was only separated from the modern beach by a few yards and a wire fence, but it was like walking on the beach fifty years earlier. Museum quality brain coral and large conch shells lay here and there stuck in the hardpan. I saw clear hand blown light bulbs and all the bottles were of the stopper variety instead of modern screw tops. There were remains of campfires and in the ashes of one were burned deer bones and a spent 45/70 rifle shell. The shell should date the occurrence to around the turn of the century.

While searching for more artifacts, we came across a partially exposed skeleton of a large fish (Fig. 5). I chipped some of the hardpan away and when it was apparent that it was not a tarpon as I first thought, I decided to collect the specimen. We went back to Walt's for some plaster, burlap, and a bucket and returned to the fish. We chiseled through the hardpan isolating the specimen and then wrapped the whole thing in a plaster bandage, not unlike one uses to support a broken leg. When I returned to the university the following week, the bandaged block joined others in the storage area. That accounts for the lag time of three years before we realized the specimen's importance.

Then, one Saturday morning, Roy Pickerell, a volunteer preparator, completed a project and came to my office asking, "What next?"

We went to the storage room and pulled out the Port Aransas block, placed it on a dolly and took it to the preparation laboratory. I returned to my office leaving Roy chipping away. Just before lunch he appeared at my office door suggesting that I come look at what he had found. When we arrived at the laboratory, there was a paper towel lying over the rock in the fish's stomach area. Roy slowly removed the towel from the tail of a small fish and I said something like: "Found his last meal, I see."

Then he jerked the towel away, exposing the front half of the small skeleton. There, to my surprise and delight, was the complete skeleton of a tiny mermaid (Fig. 6). Incredible! I have been shocked by fossils of unlikely creatures before, but always in exotic places like Egypt, never in Texas. The specimen has now been prepared and studied and is described below:

Homichthys sohli, new genus and species

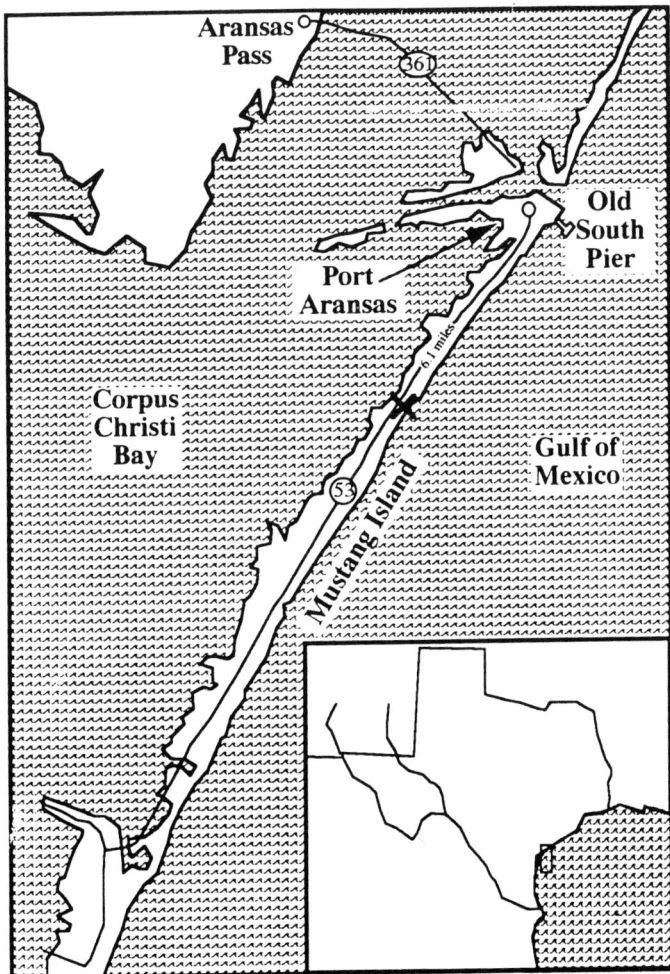

Figure 4 *Discovery site of the Atlantic Mermaid*

Figs. 5 & 6

Holotype: LU 61978, complete skeleton.

Diagnosis: Small size (25 centimeters); torso from midlength forward very hominoid but from midlength back its the tail of a teolost fish.

Etymology: Homo (human) + *ichthys* (fish)= manfish + *sohli*; named for Walter Sohl, my friend through whose curiosity specimen came to light.

Type locality: Port Aransas, Texas, 6.l miles south of the old South Pier and approximately 150 yards from high tide surf (Fig. 4).

Description: The skull, arms, and shoulders are indistinguishable from those of a modern human except for their small size. The ribs are also hominoid but the vertebrae from head to tail are amphicoelus (concave-concave) and very fishlike. There are no fins other than the caudal (tail), so stabilization during swimming must have been accomplished by the hands. The tail is essentially that of a teolost fish but its function was like that of a marine mammal (whales) in that it undulated dorso-ventrally instead of from side to side. There are no scales preserved, but I feel they were lost postmortem. There are no scales preserved with the large fish and I'm certain that it had scales. Its not uncommon for the skin and scales to slough off of a dead fish lying on the sea floor before burial.

The fish (Fig.5) is also new to science but is not described here. It is an elopid (herring) of some kind, although I know of no living elopid this large. Perhaps its a rare deep water form brought to the surface by the hurricane.

On June 12, l947, I was on the old South Pier in Port Aransas when a local fisherman, named Charlie Stella, landed a 12 foot hammerhead shark that weighed 947 pounds. Patricia Pogue, a well known ichthyologist, was also present, and she cut

9

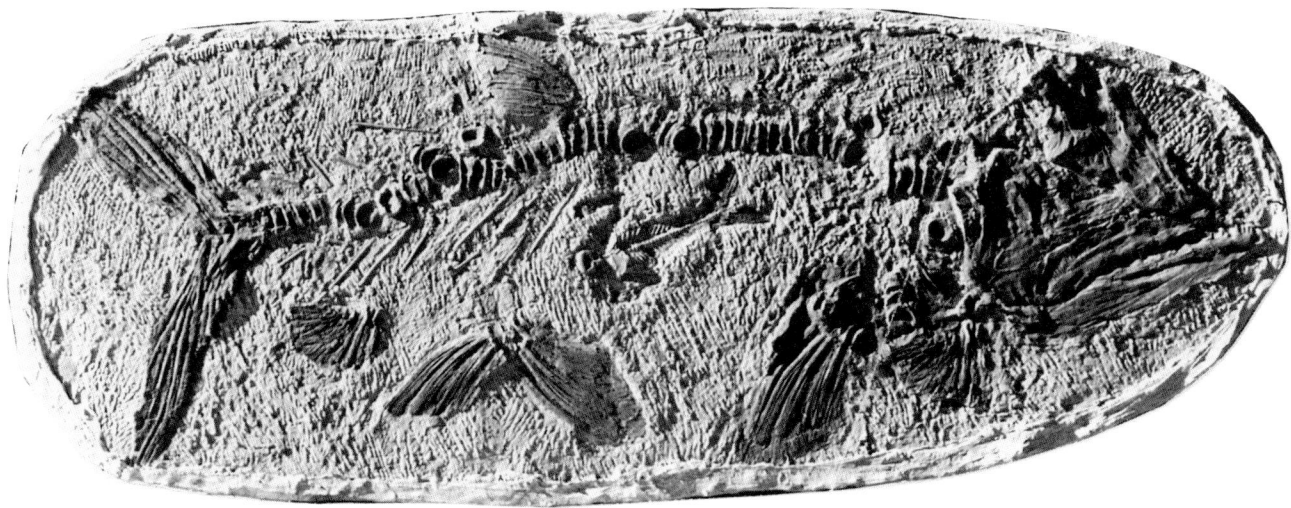

Figure 5 *Fossil fish with Atlantic Mermaid*

Figure 6 *Close up of Atlantic Mermaid*

the beast open and collected the stomach contents. The following year, I was discussing the event with Mr. Foster, owner of the South Pier Bait Stand, when he showed me a letter from Dr. Pogue listing the shark's stomach contents: Redfish, Whiting, Kingfish, Red Snapper, as well as some remains of a small goat, and an arm of an "incredibly tiny human, probably a fetus." The goat and human were attributed to floods washing them from rivers into the sea.

When I remembered the incident, I tried to locate Dr. Pogue but, alas, she had died several years earlier. I drove to Austin where she was based and inquired about her stomach analysis material. I sighed when I was shown hundreds of gallon jars, but found that they were filed by date. I had the date on the photo of Stella with his trophy catch and sure enough there it was: a jar marked JUNE 12,1947 - SOUTH PIER, PORT ARANSAS, TEXAS, 12 FOOT HAMMERHEAD.

I poured the contents out in a screen and scratched through the mess. There it was! Much of the flesh had fallen off and it certainly was no fetus. Dr. Pogue would have realized it was adult had she seen the bones. This individual is nearly twice the size of our fossil (Fig. 7), but still within the sexually dimorphic size range for a population. So it would seem that we have two occurrences of these tiny mermaids within six miles of each other, and both victims of fish. Even though they died almost a half century apart, I feel certain that there are still members of this population swimming off the Texas coast, buried in Texas beaches, and possibly inside of preserved fish in ichthyological collections.

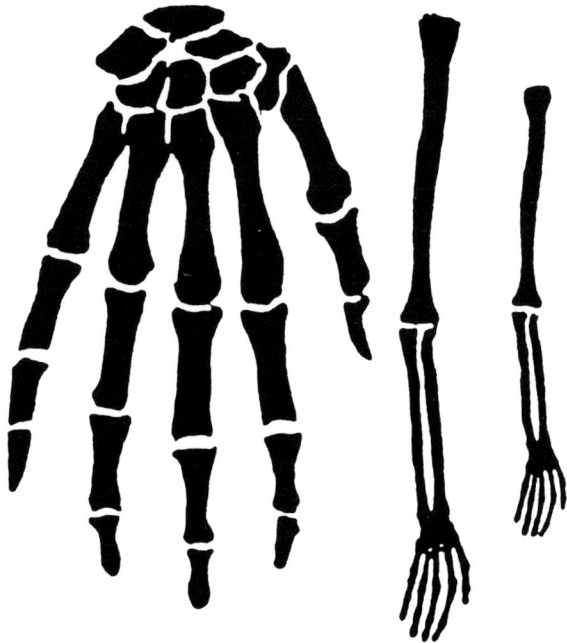

Figure 7 *Modern human hand compared with arm sizes of:*
   A. Mermaid described herein
   B. Arm of speciment found in a shark belly in 1947

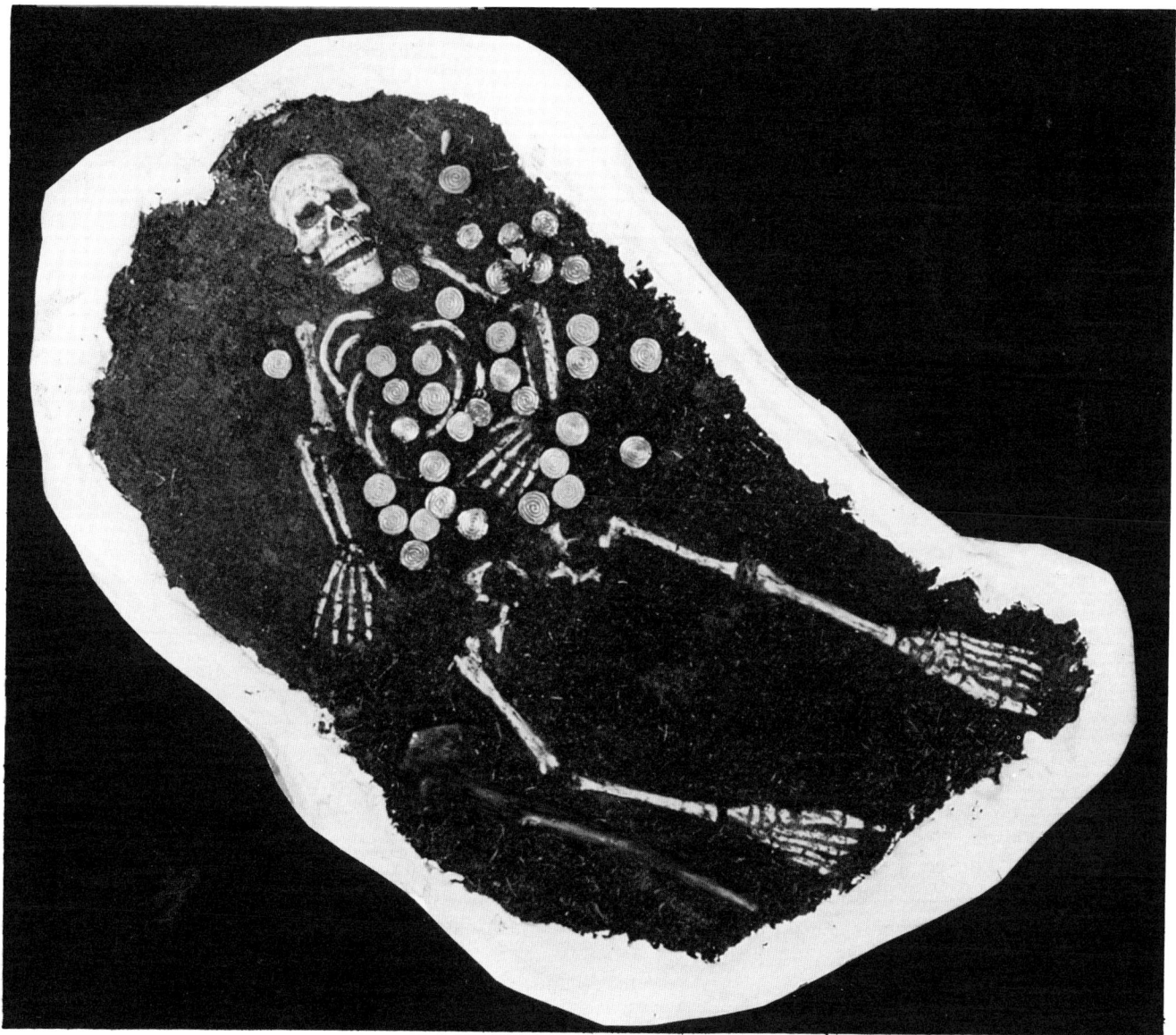

Figure 8   *Boyne River Leprechaun skeleton.*

Boyne River Leprechaun

It was Monday morning and I had just sat down at my desk when the phone rang. "Overseas operator with a call from Ireland for Professor Slaughter." My mind was racing through its filing system for someone I knew in Ireland when a voice with an Irish brogue came on the line. "Slaughter! McNeely here." I met Callen McNeely at a pub near the university where we held weekly brainstorming sessions with graduate students. He had a propensity to mention his Irish ancestry but I didn't know that he was in Ireland.

"Erin go braugh. What in the name of St.Pat are you doing over there?" I joked.

"Just bumming around and checking on my ancestors. Are you still interested in strange and unusual fossils?" he queried.

"That depends," I replied.

"How would you feel about a Leprechaun skeleton complete with his gold cache?" he answered with an Irish twinkle in his voice.

"Cal, that's a real long shot. Why not send me photographs?" I said with an air of disbelief.

"You kidding? It may not be there tomorrow. Tell you what, I'll underwrite your airline ticket and if you're disappointed, you owe me nothing."

Two afternoons later Cal met me at the Dublin airport. As we walked across the parking lot, he told me that he wanted to drive close to the site that day so we could excavate early the next morning. I could tell he was worried that someone else might find his discovery. It was dark when we drove up to the rural pub and I knew why Cal had chosen it. I could hear the laughter and music, even with the car windows rolled up. When we entered, everyone greeted him like a long lost relative. Yep, I thought, that's old Cal. After about an hour, I reminded him that he wanted to get an early start and that I was suffering from jet lag. He took me upstairs to our room and returned to the party. I could hear him telling stories in his put-on Irish accent well into the night. Nevertheless, it was he who awakened me before dawn the next morning. I could smell yesterday's booze but he was perky as usual. The innkeeper's wife had a huge breakfast waiting and it was much appreciated. As we drove away, Cal continued his story. "I was driving around just enjoying the countryside when I saw a sign, PEAT QUARRY. I drove in just to see what it was like. At the office they told me that their insurance company wouldn't allow visitors, but if I continued down the road to its end I would find a stone fence. Just on the other side of the fence I would find a number of small quarries made by the locals when they used it for fuel. I had plenty of time, so I followed instructions. Sure enough, there was an ancient stone fence. Over I went and walked about. Vegetation doesn't seem to do well on the floor of the pits so walking was easy. The peat is less than a foot thick and is covered by about the same thickness of sandy soil. They said the peat was too thin here to be of commercial value. Strolling in one of the smaller pits, I spotted a metallic glint in the sun and it turned out to be a gold coin," he said, thrusting his opened hand toward me. It was indeed a gold disk about the size of a nickel.

I put my hand lens on it and said, "Its hand made and may be quite old."

Cal continued, "The peat was slightly eroded nearby, forming a tiny canyon and there was the edge of another coin jutting from the peat. With my pocket knife I scratched at the peat, uncovering several others and then a tiny human skull. That's when I called you."

"Cal," I confided, "I'm intrigued by this and am really looking forward to meeting your little Leprechaun. Did you remember to get the plaster, burlap, and water?"

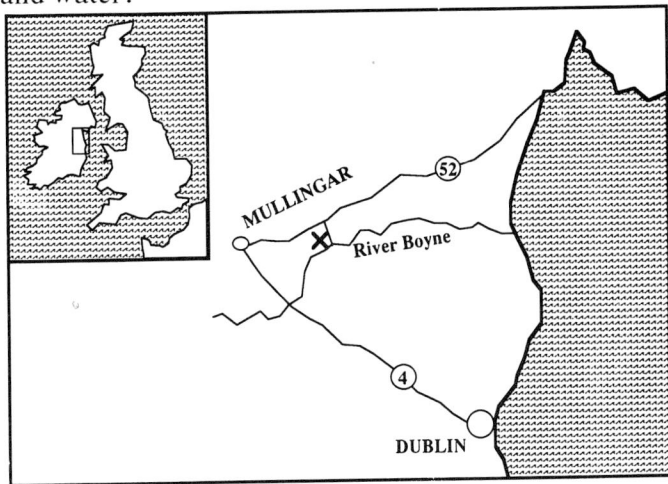

Figure 9 *Boyne River Locality map.*

"Is Ireland green?" he answered indignantly. He turned off the main road and then pointed out the commercial quarry as we passed. He drove right up to the old stone fence and there was a charming wooden style over it. We divided the equipment and materials and started off with Cal setting the pace. He nimbly jumped into one of the pits and fell to his knees. He removed a flat rock he had placed over his excavation and began sweeping the sand and loose peat from the fossil. The sun was up now and it reflected on the gold disks he had uncovered.

"Cal, I'm amazed that you were able to leave all this gold unattended."

"Hell, you know I'm more interested in knowledge than money." he said, a bit ruffled.

Minimal scratching proved the skeleton to be essentially complete, so I decided to plaster the specimen without completely exposing it. We dug a trench through the six inch lens of peat and wrapped the whole thing in a plaster bandage. The whole block weighed less than forty pounds so I fashioned a rope handle and checked it through with my luggage. I thought it would have less chance to be lost this way and I also wanted to be there when it went through U.S.Customs. I won't go into the hassle at customs about opening the block but I did finally get it to the university. The specimen has now been prepared but left in place in the peat. I submit the following description and discussion below. A new species of modern man is proposed, but when enough individuals are found, it may be more appropriate to reduce the taxon to subspecies.

Homo mcneelyi, new species
(Fig. 8)

Holotype: LU 62666. Complete male skeleton.

Diagnosis: Small size (about 18 inches tall); hands and feet unusually large.

Type locality: East side of th River Boyne, 15.7 kilometers east of Mullinger, County of Heath (Fig. 9); south end of quarry.

Etymology: Named in honor of Callen McNeely for his Irish heart and his curious mind.

Description: The skeleton represents a middle age male who stood about eighteen inches tall. His mouth is rather large and he has outsized hands and feet. The teeth are in excellent condition

15

for a man his age. The smallest modern human recorded is a female that stood 19 inches tall, only one inch taller than our Leprechaun. However, the odds against the discovery of an ancient skeleton of our species smaller than any recorded, would be incredibly high. The probability of our Leprechaun being near the normal size for the population is great.

Discussion: There are no clasps, buttons, etc. associated to give us a hint of the garb of the Leprechaun. There is a stick that has been smoothed and polished adjacent to his right leg (Fig.8). The right tibia (lower leg bone) was broken and almost mended so I suspect the stick was used as a cane. It seems rather heavy for a cane and may have been used as a weapon as well. If so, this is by far the oldest shillelagh known from Ireland. The age of the fossil is fairly certain from several lines of evidence. A radiocarbon date was run on some of the surrounding peat and the results indicated an age of 3580 plus/minus 50 years. That translates to between 2120 and 1770 B.C. In Ireland this would be near the beginning of the Bronze Age. A pollen analysis was also performed and oak pollen was found to outnumber elm pollen three to one. The extensive elm forests of Ireland began to dwindle about 3500 B.C. and oak trees took up the slack in the pollen profile. This supports the radiocarbon date, but could the Leprechaun have been buried in the peat much later?

  The spirals that decorate the gold disks also decorate the ancient "passage" tombs of the Beaker People, who arrived in Ireland not long before the transition between the Stone Age and the Bronze Age. The oldest Beaker graves contain no metal but about 2000 B.C. they made wrought objects of gold and copper. Still later they learned enough metallurgy to cast bronze. Since the Stone Age gave way to metal about 2000 B.C., our leprechaun must be no older the wrought gold disks (?coins). He's probably not much younger, however, because of the lack of bronze objects. This supports the radiocarbon date and means the individual was either buried or fell into the bog about 4,000 years ago. If these gold disks were indeed used as coins, they would be by far the oldest since proper coinage heretofore was not known older than about 500 B.C. This makes the leprechaun the oldest known fossil of fringe hominoids in Europe. It also has some bearing on the origin of Leprechauns. It has usually been held that Leprechauns took origin from Scandinavian Gnomes who came to Ireland with the first Viking raiders. We now know, however, that they were in Ireland nearly 2,000 years before the Vikings arrived around 700 B.C. The Beaker People apparently arrived in Ireland about the same time as the Leprechauns. Passage tombs similar to those the Beakers decorated with carved spirals have been found in northwestern Iberia (Spain and Portugal) and it is presumed that this is the area from which the Beaker People came. The Galicia area of northwestern Iberia not only has Beaker-type tombs but this is the home of folk tales of the Eunano, small people of the forest. It seems possible that some *Eunano* accompanied the Beakers to Ireland and evolved into the *Leprechauns*.

Bunyips

I was pleased to find a large envelope in my mail box at the University with the return address of Hugh McCormick. I first met Hugh when he was doing graduate work on early mammals at Columbia University. After graduation, he moved to Australia mainly because he felt that many secrets of evolution were to be found there. Since his move, I occasionally received copies of his publications, but we really had not had a chance to talk. I was therefore pleased to find a letter in this most recent packet of reprints.

Dear Bob: Last time we met at the Society of Vertebrate Paleontology meetings, you said that you planned a trip to Australia. That was years ago and I'm still waiting. Perhaps after you read this letter you will come. I've been keeping up with your quest for fossil fringe hominoids and I have found one.

One day last spring a mammalogist interested in bats brought me a map indicating a cave in southwestern Australia which was not on our register. I visited the cave to evaluate its fossil potential. Near the entrance of the cave, beneath a low ledge, I found a few bones that appear to be human. I plastered out a block that contains two skulls. One is a Tasmanian Devil and the other is a hominoid of relatively small size for an adult. The skull appears to be fairly typical Homo erectus but the deposit is clearly not old enough for that fossil species. The teeth are not homonoid but lophodont like those of a grazer (kangaroo). Call me if you'd like to borrow the specimen.

Sincerely,
Hugh

It should go without saying that I sent a request to see the unusual specimen post haste. When it arrived I immediately set to work exposing the minutae of the teeth for examination. Although it's very clear that the teeth belong to the skull, their structure is that of a grass/leaf eater as Hugh had said. He had not mentioned, however, that the single premolar was of a sheering type only known in certain marsupials. Another important feature is that our fossil has only one incisor in each jaw quadrant whereas humans and apes have two. Not only are the teeth of modern humans fairly

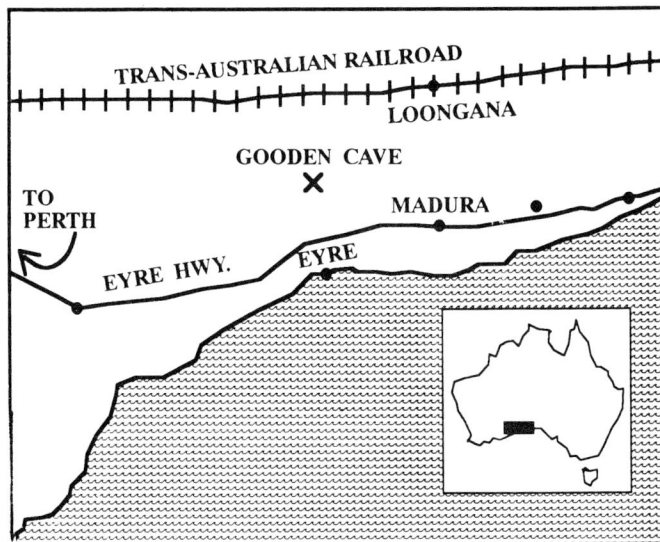

Figure 10 *Bunyip locality map.*

Figure 11 *Partial skeleton of a Bunyip.*

consistent in form, but so are those of known relatives in the distant past. One half of this specimen lay on its side in the cave sediment and as I scratched at it for more detail, I was shocked to discover the symphyses of the lower jaws are not fused. The two halves of the lower jaw are separate in most mammals, joined by connecting tissue only. This allows more mobility in side action while chewing. In primates, pigs, camels, horses, and a vew few other mammals, this symphysis is fused to give added strength to the bite. Furthermore this jaw has an inflected angle on the posterior edge, a character that is this well developed in marsupials. If we had only the lower jaws of this creature, we would consider the form to be a short-faced grazing animal, probably a kangaroo.

With this realization, I quickly examined the pelvic area partially exposed at one corner of the block. There it was, a pre-pubis bone known only in marsupials. I hesitated to even consider this new evidence but since the teeth are kangaroo-like, vacuities, and prepubis bone seems to leave little doubt that we have a man-like marsupial. By normal evolution standards, a human-like marsupial would have to be seperate from the placental primates in general, which can only be traced back some sixty million years. In light of the evidence there appear to be only two possible explanations. First, these creatures are similar to humans through convergent evolution. That is, they look similar because both evolved the best set of features for the same environmental situation. . . i.e., no relationship. Or, secondly, the creature evolved in another situation (extraterrestrial?) where the rules

19

are different. Although it is possible that an early hominoid could have acquired the marsupial-like characteristics exhibited by this creature, the truth probably could only be answered by the DNA hybridization procedure. Dr. Gil King, Director of the King Forensic and Genetic Laboratories, agreed to see if he could recover enough material to run the procedure. I gathered as much bone scrap as I could be certain belonged to this individual and hand-delivered it to his lab eighty miles away. When he called a week later, I held my breath.

"Its clearly not human. In fact I can't match it to any group in my meager collection of primates," Gill said.

I hesitated to make such a suggestion but timidly asked, "Do you have any samples of marsupials?"

"You must be kidding." Gil replied, "All I have is an opossum."

"If its not too much trouble, compare the creature to the opossum and I'll send you a piece of a kangaroo bone. I'll tell you why later."

Without going into detail, I'll just report that the DNA and protein sequences of our creature are more similar to the oppossum than to human, horse, or other familiar animals. The DNA of a tree kangaroo I sent was even more similar. So it is very clear that we are dealing with a new order of mammals.

When I expressed my ideas to Gil, he asked, "Why are they so rare and where is their fossil record?"

"Read my book," is all I could answer.

I published a preliminary note on my findings in Aussie Science Magazine. Soon I received several letters suggesting that our beast was clearly a *Bunyip*, a creature "imagined" by Aboriginals and some rural Australians. I surveyed the meager literature and located the formost authority on the *Bunyip*, one James Shutte. When I contacted Dr.

Shutte, he was adamant that such creatures still exist.

"I've just completed a book on one human *Bunyip* encounter," he said. "They are about three quarters the size of an Aboriginal Australian, covered with reddish fur, except for the face, have excellent night vision and apparently are silent. They have only four toes. Their general body shape is that of a small human and mothers carry their young in a pouch, like marsupials."

He knew little of their teeth. Our specimen is incomplete and disarticulated so the feature of four toes cannot be determined. The specimen does have eye sockets that are slightly larger than usual which may be consistant with Shutte's night vision observation. The presence of a pouch is reinforced by the presence of a pre-pubis bone (marsupial) in our skeleton. This creature is clearly a marsupial and not a human. It only appears humanoid because it evolved over a long period of time under conditions that allowed it to occupy a niche similar to that of early primates.

Homoides marsupialus, new genus and species
Fig. 11

Type specimen: Skull, right and left humerus and ulna-radius, ribs, and one femur No.365-33743 (Fig. 11), Lundelius Institute of Paleontology, Perth, Western Australia.

Diagnosis: Skull superficially resembles that of a primitive human; symphyses unfused and teeth lophodont for eating coarse vegetation. There is only one large incisor in each jaw quadrant (1/1), no canines (0/0), one shearing premolar (1/1), two molars (2/2). Compare this dental formula, 1-0-1-2, to that of hominids and apes, 2-1-2-3. On the other hand the dentition is very similar to that of a tree kangaroo. The marsupial characters of pre-pubis bone and palatal vacuities are also present.

Type locality: Gooden Cave on the Craig Gooden Station, sixty miles east of the town of Ballafonia, north of the Eyre Highway, Southwestern Australia (Fig. 10).

Etymology: Homoides indicates superficial similarity to humans + marsupialus to indicate the creature's Infraclass affinities = Manlike Marsupial.

Discussion: Associated with the skeleton of the *Bunyip* are the bones of a Tasmanian Devil

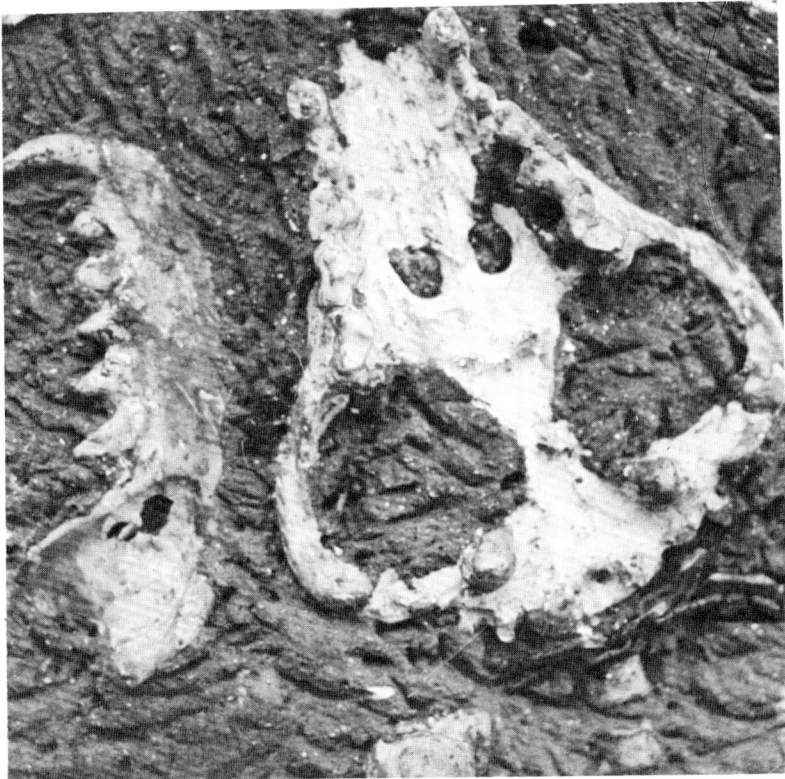

Figure 12 *Skull of Tasmanian Devil.*

(Sarchophilus), a small carnivorous marsupial about the size of a raccoon (Fig.12). A solid silver chain is in such a position as to leave no doubt it was around the Devil's

neck. These small carnivores can hold their own against enemies somewhat larger than themselves but their appearance is very cuddly and I'm not surprised that they were kept as pets by the *Bunyip.* This does, however, add a very human-like quality to the *Bunyip* behavior.

Almost certainly *Bunyips* had their entire evolution in Australia, like so many unusual animals that survived there through the lack of competition with similar creatures with a more competitive nature. That such hominoids could evolve twice from very different stock gives credence to the idea that if the human race were wiped out, their niche would be refilled given enough time.

Figure 13 *Fairy skeleton, female (left) and male (right).*

Cliff End Fairies

Jwas in England with my associate, Dr. Wayne Amerine, to prospect for fossil mammals of Lower Cretaceous age. The Wealden Formation underlies much of southern England and is the right age for important fossils. On our initial visit to the British Museum, Dr. George Black, a curator, invited us to join him for lunch at the Bunch of Grapes Pub on Brompton Road. We rolled out the maps between pints of lager and kidney pies, and began recording outcrops he knew in southern England. He then suggested that we contact Jill Alexander of Coventry.

"She's an avid fossil buff and probably knows many outcrops unknown to me," he told us.

We called Alexander, and she was anxious to help. She even offered to drive us to the Hastings-Rye area on the southeast coast. It was this area that had produced most of the fossils of the desired age in her collection. She picked us up at the train station and we went to her house to see her collection. While I was looking over her extensive collection, I came across a slab of mudstone with the distinct impression of the tip of a huge insect wing. I know of no insect this large younger than the Permian period and there are no rocks of such antiquity around here. Nevertheless, Jill said that she found this specimen at the foot of a cliff of Wealden deposits between Hastings and Rye. We decided to take off a few days from mammal hunting to see if we could get enough of

this insect to identify. To save time, and wear and tear on Jill's small car, we took a train to Hastings where we rented a small station wagon and with Jill as our guide, we drove to Cliff End (Fig.14). The cliff is very sheer and faces the sea. Normal wave action doesn't reach the cliff but during storms the cliff is sometimes undercut, causing slides of rock, sand, and clay. It was in one such rubble pile that the wing tip was found. I scanned the cliff above the slide with my binoculars. The cliff was made up of mostly soft, sandy clay and coarse sandstone. Then, there it was, a thin lenticular deposit of dark mudstone at the very top of the cliff, only a foot or two below the modern surface. Nevertheless, it was far too dangerous to try to reach the lens from the top. We picked up a few pieces of the same rock from the rubble pile and some contained leaf impressions.

Jill introduced us to the proprietor of a pub down the road where we rented two very pleasant upstairs rooms. He even loaned us a wheelbarrow and an extra shovel. Four of the pub patrons volunteered their services and met us the next morning at the parking area east of the cliff. We attacked the rubble pile from the sea side, examining every piece of rock and shoveling the sand and clay away. After two days we'd found nothing but impressions of leaves and one flower. Our crew shrunk to Jill, Wayne and myself. I even began to suspect that Jill was beginning to think of better things to do. Just when our morale was at its lowest ebb, Jill, perched at the apex of the pile, let out a shout, "Bones! I've got bones!"

Wayne and I scrambled up to help her drag the two by three foot slab of rock down. It was covered with mud but we could easily see a number of

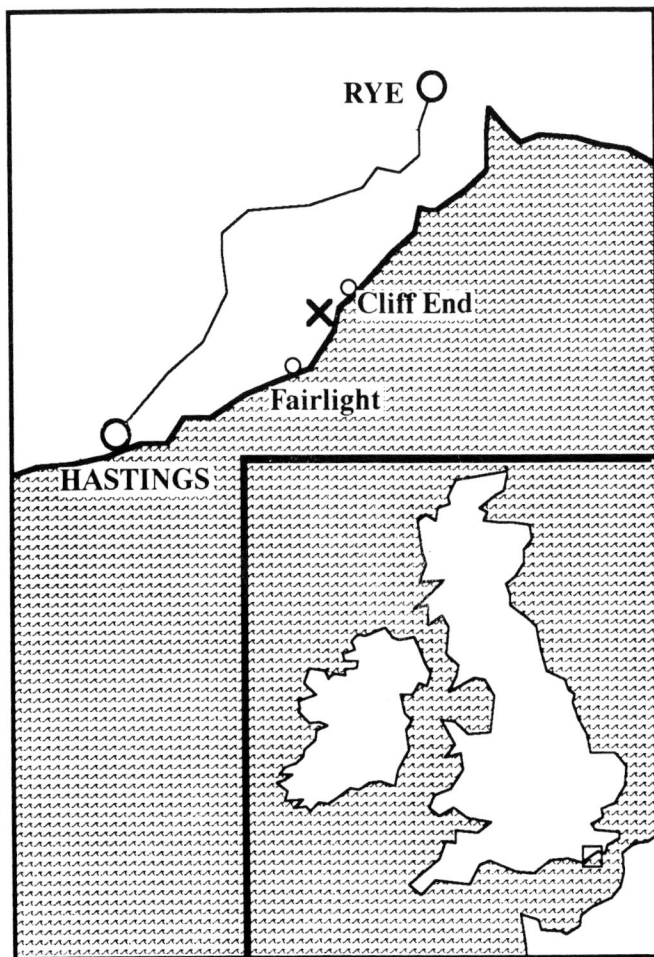

Figure 14 *Cliff End Fairy locality.*

small, embedded bones. I carried the slab a couple hundred yards to the edge of the calm sea, submerged it and began to wash the mud from its surface. As the water cleared we were all so aghast that no one spoke for a minute. There was one partial, and two complete skeletons of what appeared to be tiny humans. Even more amazing were impressions of large "insect" wings positioned in such a way as to leave little doubt that they belonged to these tiny people.

Jill broke the silence with, "I say, I do believe we've discovered a flock of fairies."

We continued to move rubble for a couple more hours but my heart was not in it. I was too anxious to get back to London to finish cleaning the specimen and show it to our friends and colleagues. Jill very generously turned the specimen over to us with the promise that we would send her a cast. The specimen (Fig.13) has now been prepared and studied enough for a preliminary description.

Homopteryx nanus, new genus and species
Fig. 13

Holotype : LUM 62773, Complete female skeleton with wing impressions.

Paratype : LUM 62774, Complete male skeleton with wing impressions.

Diagnosis: Small size (358 millimeters) ; presence of insect-like wings; lacks fibula; sternum ossified.

Etymology: *Homo* (human) + *pteryx* (winged) + *nanus* (tiny) = Tiny Winged People.

Type locality: Cliff End near Fairlight, between Hastings and Rye, southeast England (Fig.14), 325 yards west of the end of the sea wall.

Horizon: Thin (one to three inch) lens of gray mudstone near the top of the cliff.

Age: Some woody stems were submitted for radiocarbon dating but proved to be too young for a meaningful date. The one abundant plant associated is Evening Primrose, which is a New World plant imported to England in the early 1600's. A few decades probably passed before there were widespread wild stands of the plant.

The surface hasn't changed much since the small pond was open and filled with water. It therefore was on the slope of the land to the sea. I guesstimate that the pond filled with sediments in the late 17th Century or early 18th Century. Since that time, the Cliff retreat has been great enough to bisect the deposit.

Discussion: Features used to sex modern human skeletons (i.e. brow ridges, pelvic shape, etc.) indicates that the complete skeletons represent one male and one female. The partial skeleton is probably a female also. Their insect-like wings are so different that some zoologists might insist that they belong to different species. Considering their proximity and the rarity of fossil fairies, I reject this view. Instead, I feel certain that this is a case of extreme sexual dimorphism. Some fish and birds reduce or eliminate competition between the sexes by evolving very different lifestyles, sometimes to the point that teeth and other anatomical features are very different. This can allow them to nearly double their population size. I feel that this the case for this species of fairy.

Drawing from analogy, as we often do, the moth-like wings of the female may suggest that they were/are nocturnal, while the dragonfly-like wings may suggest the males were diurnal. This could mean that fraternization between the sexes would most likely be restricted to periods around dusk or dawn. This hypothesis is supported by the impressions of fully opened Evening Primrose blossoms in the same rock. This flower only blooms at dusk. In addition, the single insect (Fig.16) preserved as a negative mold in the rock is a firefly which spends the daylight hours beneath

Figure 15 *Amerine examining fossils.*

26

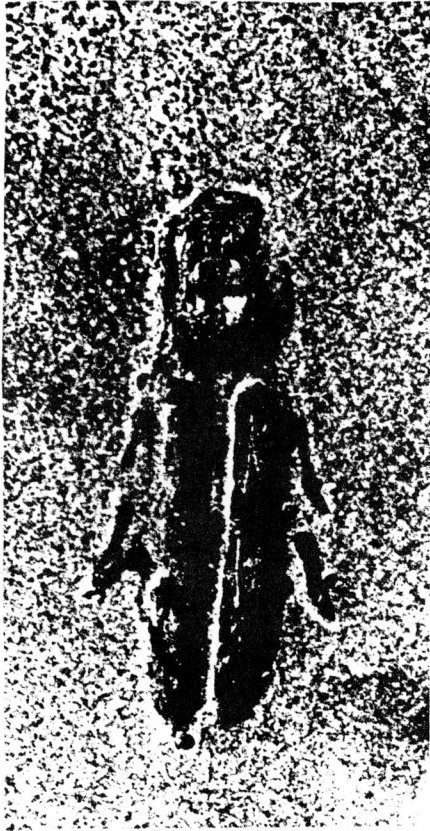

Figure 16 *Fossil firefly.*

flown to higher ground. Perhaps a sudden violent windstorm threw them into the water where the semi-rigid wings would be a distinct handicap. This could also explain the presence of leaves and flowers of Evening Primrose removed from their stems and deposited in the pond. The extent of the catastrophe remains unknown, but three individuals buried in such a short time frame suggests there may have been many more. As no other fossils of these creatures have been reported, they must be very rare, or their accidental burial a very unlikely and rare occurrence.

he bark of trees and emerges at dusk.

    Mortality: I am hard-pressed to determine the cause of death and burial of these individuals. No bones are broken and even the gossamer wings seem to be in perfect condition. Still, the sudden demise of at least three individuals negates the possibility of natural death (old age or disease). Flood seems unlikely as the sediment size remains very fine, and besides, they could have easily have

27

DESANDERS GNOME

y wife, Juliana, returned to the living room after a raucous phone call. "What did Judy have to say?" I inquired.
"How did you know it was Judy?"
"Laughter and glass talk. Simple, my dear Watson."
"Judy is in Germany doing a tour studying the glass paintings. She says that she has something for you that'll blow your mind," Juliana said.

The real story didn't unfold until Judy DeSanders, glass artist extraordinary, returned two weeks later. We picked her up at the airport and in spite of travel fatigue, she led us straight to the bar. She handed me a heavy package wrapped in brown paper but told me not to open it until she had finished her story.

"We were in the small village of Lahr on the banks of the Rhine River and at the edge of the Black Forest (Fig. 17). The local people opened their homes to us and I was staying with a couple at the edge of town. I had a most pleasant roomie, one Alice Rosell, a glass artist from England. Our hosts were pleasant people but spoke almost no English. Fortunately, Alice spoke pretty good German. I often told her we must visit Mexico together so I could translate for her.

"No glass trips planned for Saturday, some of us made our way to some Celtic ruins nearby. There was a tomb and I was delighted when I saw that some of the fired bricks that made up a retaining wall at the entrance, had spirals on them. I remem-bered our discussion about spirals being used in Spain and Ireland in association with ancient peoples and *Leprechauns*. I made an offhand statement that I'd sure like to have one of those bricks and everyone looked at me like a leper. Antiquity laws, you know... I was scolded. So, I took a few pictures to show you and that was that."

I realized then that Judy had somehow managed to get her hands on a Celtic brick and started to open the package, but Judy put her hand on mine and said:

"Not yet. Story isn't finished. That evening Alice told our hosts about the day and apparently mentioned my lust for one of the Celtic bricks. The lady of the house said that an ancestor built a farmhouse nearby back in the 17th or 18th century. It burned during WWII but the chimney was still standing. The hearth was made of Celtic brick they had collected from somewhere near there and

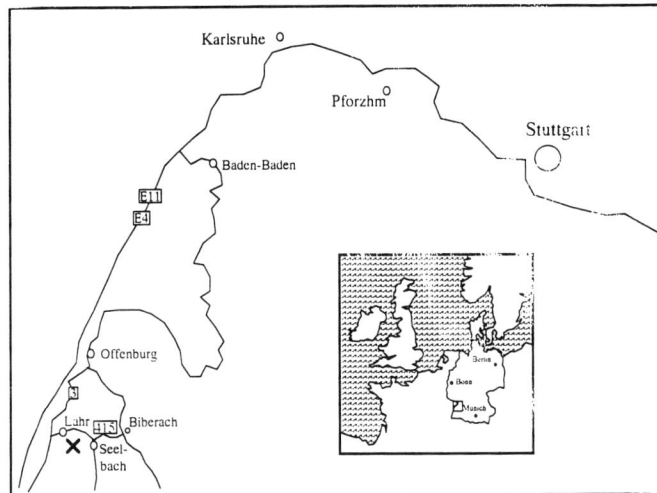

Figure 17 *Desanders Gnome locality map.*

Figure 18 *DeSanders Gnomes bones*

perhaps we could retrieve one or two of those.

"Sunday morning we visited the old ruins of her ancestors' house and sure enough the stone chimney was still standing tall. The hearth had not fared as well and the Celtic bricks were in a pile, some nearly melted away. As I was going through them looking for one with a spiral, I found one that was split lengthwise and in the broken face were charred bones."

With that, she gave me the nod to open the package.

The brick was pretty much as advertised. The broken surface presented bones that were charred black by the firing heat. They obviously had been placed in the clay before firing. The brick also presented several spirals that apparently decorated the brick mold. She said that the broken bricks that had no spirals contained no bones but fragments of bricks with spirals always had evidence of bones and that she had more of these broken bricks on the way.

The thing that thrilled me about the discovery was that our specimen has a crushed and charred skull that clearly was the size and general shape of the one (Fig. 18) we had recovered near the Boyne River in Ireland. In fact, we surely must consider this the same species or subspecies. For future discussion, this specimen will be known as the *DeSanders Gnome*.

A radiocarbon date run on some of the broken bone indicated an age of 4,200 years +/-250 before present. That is very close to the dates recorded for the *Boyne River Leprechaun*.

I have already speculated that some of the small *Eunano* people of Iberia had accompanied the Beaker People to Ireland about 4,000 years ago, and that these *Eunano* became the *Leprechauns*. I have also suggested that some *Eunano* may have accompanied the Iberians (Celts) to Northern Europe where they became the *Gnomes*. Celtic legend holds that Iberia is their area of origin. Judy's discovery certainly supports this hypothesis, even though it muddies the nomenclature a little. Instead of the Boyne River specimen representing a *Leprechaun*, it must be considered an incipient *Leprechaun* and the *DeSanders Gnome* is actually an incipient *gnome*. Furthermore, the *Boyne River Leprechaun* is so similar as to be considered the same species, if not the same population. It's my guess that the *Boyne River Leprechaun* and the *DeSanders Gnome* probably would be indistinguishable from the *Eunanos* if we could find an example of the latter.

Once their gene flow had been interrupted by the English Channel, the Irish and Northern European populations went their own evolutionary way. Both groups underwent considerable size reduction either through natural or cultural selection. Reconstruction of modern *Leprechauns* via descriptions by those who have sighted same indicate that, while diminishing in size considerably, they maintained normal limb/body ratios. The sightings of *gnomes*, however, universally indicate that their limbs became somewhat shorter relative to skull and trunk size. Comparison of the *Boyne River Leprechaun* with the three examples of *DeSanders Gnomes* demonstrates this shortening of the limbs relative to the skulls in the *Gnomes*. This may indicate the beginning of the differentiation.

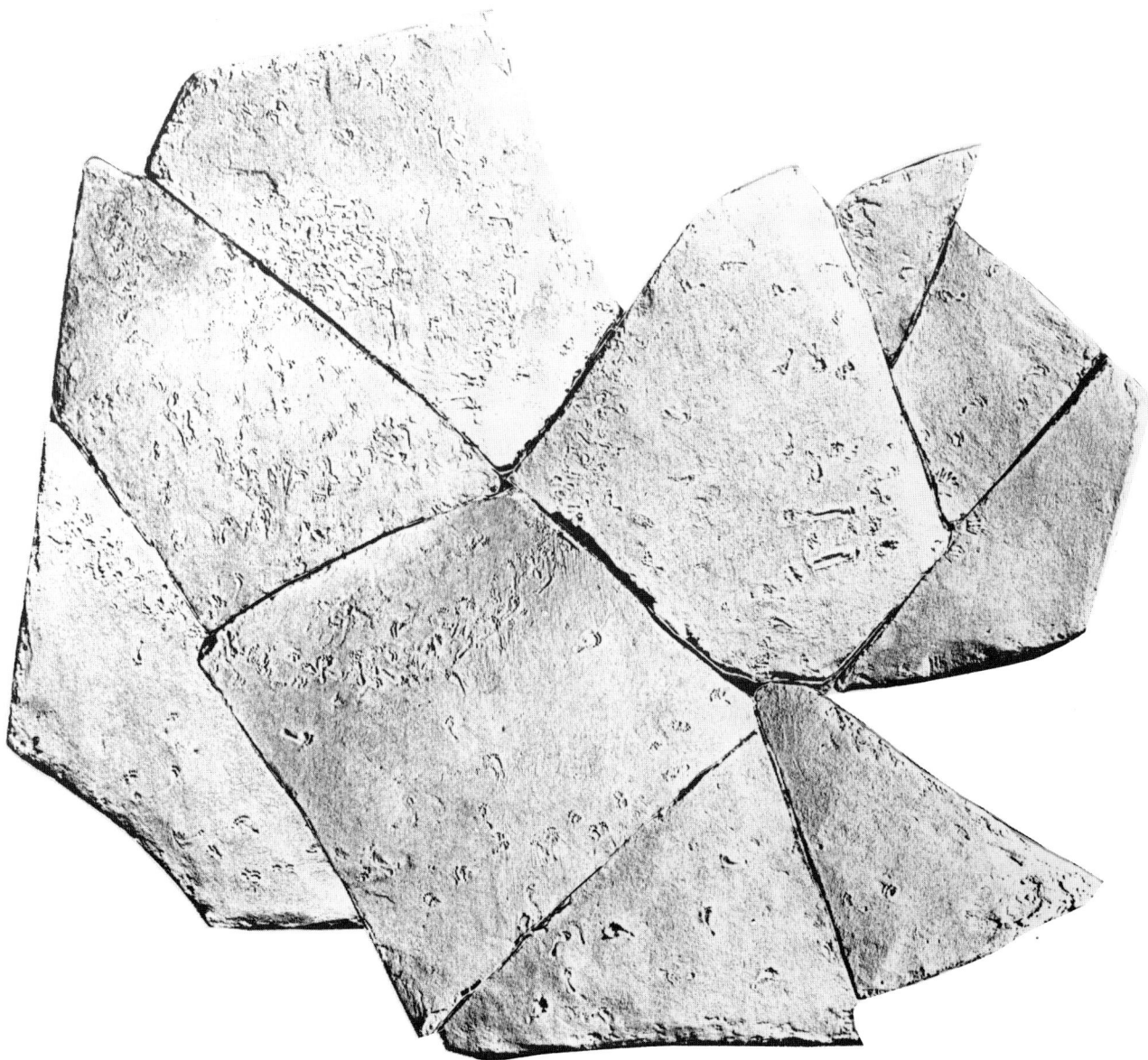

Figure 19 *Dance of the Duendes.*

32

DUENDES

In 1983 I was visiting some friends at UNAM (Univ. of Mexico) in Mexico City. Dr. Shelly Applegate, a paleoichthyologist who specializes in fossil sharks was going to take us to visit the Tapexi lithographic limestone quarry, which is south of Mexico City. The quarry is fast becoming one of the more important fossil localities in the New World. It is of Cretaceous age and has produced a huge collection of fossil fish, reptiles, and marine invertebrates. After showing us some of the collection, Dr. Applegate told us he had about an hour of work that had to be done before we left and turned us over to Miguel Angel Cabral, student preparator. Miguel speaks perfect English and we quickly discovered a common interest in fossil footprints. When Miguel showed me a collection of footprints of camels, deer, and a large cat from a Pliocene deposit, I promised to send him casts of some prints from Texas formations of similar age (5,000,000 years before present). As the deposit is near the Tapexi quarry (Fig. 20), I invited him to join us on the trip.

The drive was about four hours and our conversation covered a myriad of subjects. At one point, Shelly turned to Miguel and asked, "Have you told Slaughter about the tracks of *Duendes* dancing?"

I also addressed Miguel, "So you're holding out on me?"

Miguel, hastily and defensivly, added, "That's what the workers at the quarry call them, but they're really just tracks of kids playing. The do have some antiquity, however, in that the tracks and surrounding matrix has lithified by what I take to be freshwater marl. The quarry is in a box canyon and the rainwater that comes in the canyon via several low waterfalls percipitates its carbonates out when it mixes with the warmer pool water. This cements the sand grains together, making a sort of sandstone.

"What in the name of the Aztec Nation is a *Duende*?" I asked.

Shelly answered, "The Indians who work at the quarry have told us the *Duendes* are small people about two feet tall who come out from hiding when it rains and dance in the nude". Even a trackway of playing children intrigued me and I insisted that the site be put on our agenda. Every time Shelly or I would mention the Duende tracks, Miguel would counter with "tracks of playing children."

At long last we reached the site about thirty yards from the canyon wall and a low waterfall. The area was pretty much covered with a thin sand deposit with the "marl" deposit only showing through here and there. Miguel pointed out that the gradient was so low the sand deposits between the pools were constantly being rearranged by water and wind. Nevertheless, he used a pushbroom to expose a few of the small tracks. They did indeed look human, but I had seen fossil human tracks in Kenya, of both adults and children, and these don't look like the tracks of children. Besides, there is a rather complicated pattern to the trackways. As more and more of the footprints came to light, I turned to Miguel and said "I'd like to support your

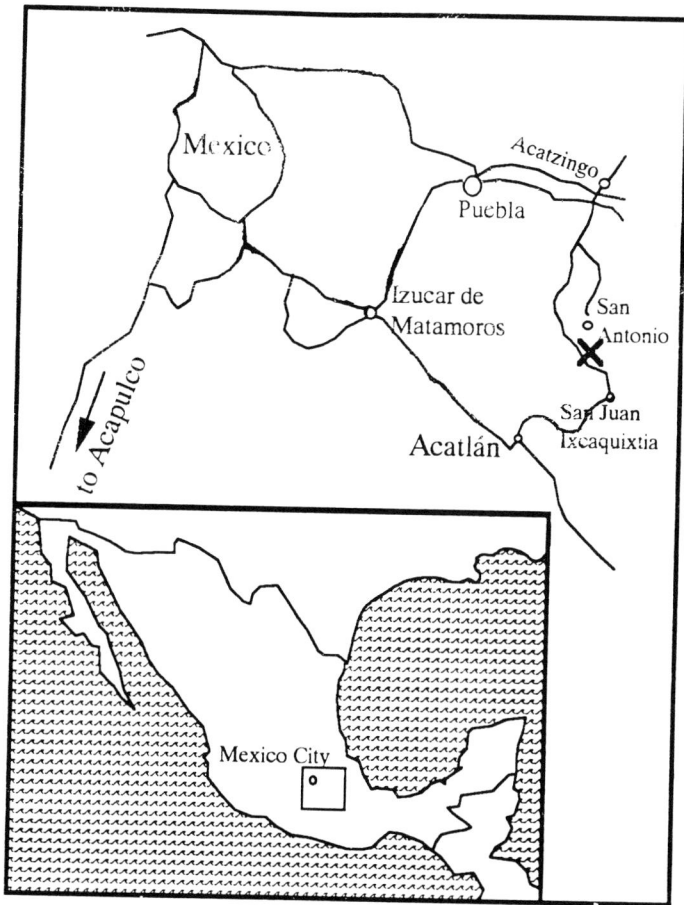

Figure 20 *Duende locality*

"playing children" hypothesis, Miguel, but I fear I'll have to look elsewhere for my explanation." Shelly smiled and nodded his approval. After Shelly arranged permission to remove the tracks, we purchased several more brooms and set to the task of uncovering all the tracks we could find. The more we uncovered, the more evident it became that there was a pattern. I could certainly see where the Indians got the idea they were *Duendes* dancing. We then marked the edges of the flags where they touched others and numbered each flag so the trackway could be rearranged in its original pattern. Back at the university we arranged the flags as they were originally and I photographed them. We interviewed some of the workers but could learn no more than we had heard, except the *Duende* were mischievous and could cause bad luck. This was part of the reason no one was anxious to talk about *Duendes*. Another important reason, however, is the fact that its considered unchristian to even see such pagan creatures.

I submitted my photographs (Fig.19) to Professor Nathan Montoya, a well known choreographer in the Dance Division at Southern Methodist University asking for any suggestions he might have. In a few days I received the following letter:

Dear Professor Slaughter: Thank you for the photographs and diagrams. The flags are indeed, an incredible find!

My colleague, Dr. Shelley Berg, and I have analyzed the tracks and have come to the following conclusions: the tracks seem to represent a primitive form of ritual circle dance. It would appear that the participants converged on the site from diverse directions. We were able to detect four radial lines of approach. Our speculation is that the dancers (most probably numbering between 5 and 10) began in a tight cluster, rotating counter-

34

clockwise at a slow, walking pace. As speed of rotation increased, the cluster began to expand and loosen in form. Individuals then proceeded by way of two consecutive steps, rotating clockwise on their own vertical axes as they moved into a distinct ring formation. The dancers then continued their individual clockwise rotations as they traveled with larger steps and occasional skips in a counter-clockwise direction, around the ring. The participants next moved through two coinsecutive hops or skips (note 'double' foot impressions, first right, then left) into a new ring of greater dimension than the first, wherein the movements were still larger and consisted of a mixture of stepping and skipping. This eventually expanded through a turning leap into a third orbit in which the sole mode of travel was skipping, largely on the balls of the feet. We observe that at least one individual lost equilibrium and fell upon landing from a leaping transition (note hand impressions). It is clear, from the angle of travel between orbits, that the entire formation moved in a continual counter-clockwise direction. It is also clear, from the distance between footprints, that the speed of the movements increased as the dance progressed from the center outward. Off hand, I would guess that this was quite a joyful or ecstatic dance.

I hope this analysis will be of some help to you. Thank you so much for letting me share in this remarkable discovery!

Sincerely,
Nathan Montoya

I phoned Dr. Applegate and reported Professor Montoya and Dr. Berg's analysis and he said "I could have guessed it."

"Guessed what?" I countered.

"That they danced counter-clockwise. The Aztecs often danced counter-clockwise just to bug the Spanish priests. Dancing counter-clockwise was considered paganistic by Christians of the period. Of course, I'm quite sure the *Duendes* were pagans in the Christian view."

There are several variations on the human footprint, no doubt representing different individuals. I made accurate drawings of these types and submitted them to the Dr. Thomas MacCaslin, authority on human footprints and protege of the late Dr. Louise Robbins, well known Forensic Anthropologist at the University of North Carolina (Greensburo). I didn't tell him that the drawings were actual size but posed the question, "Could you estimate the age of the track makers as well as their height and weight?"

Dr. MacCaslin replied, "The arches are much too well developed for young children. I would say the tracks represent individuals fifteen years or older. Each track you submitted belongs to a different individual and all are rather tall and thin, although well within a size range for a single population and race."

I quickly answered his letter, " I feel bad about not telling you that the drawings are actual size but I wanted to be sure that your judgement, concerning the age of the individuals, was not biased. I apologize but let me hasten to say that I feel certain you are correct in your interpretation." I told him that a number of us believed the trackway to be that of a group of Duendes dancing and sent him a copy of Montoya's report on the choregraphy. "Now that you know the size and circumstances could you estimate the size and weight of these little people?" His analysis follows:

Dear Professor Slaughter: I'm sure as a vetebrate paleontologist, you are aware that as the size of an animal (or hominoid) doubles, its weight cubes. If my formulae work when scaled down this far, your little *Duendes* would average from about twenty to thirty inches tall. It is indicated that they all are rather slender and probably weighed no more than fifteen to twenty pounds. I must say, I know of no adult humans this small, living or fossil. Of course, not having seen the tracks or knowing the circumstances, I'll have to reserve judgement concerning the authenticity of the prints.

Cordially,
Thomas MacCaslin

When I read Dr.MacCaslin's size estimate of the *Duende*, 20"to 24", I suddenly realized that they were very similar in size to the Boyne River incipient *Leprechaun* and the *Desander Gnome*. With this realization, it seems very possible that *Duendes*, like the *Leprechauns* and *Gnomes*, originated from the *Eunano* of Spain. They could have come to Mexico as stow-aways on Spanish sailing ships during the early part of the 16th Century. After all, the word *Duende* is Spanish, not Nahuatle. If so, the *Eunano* of Iberia were as important to the peopling of Europe and the New World with fringe hominoids as the Celts were in spreading their genes far and wide over the same areas.

Figure 21 *Author descending intoFayoud Cave.*

n 1972 I was visiting the American University of Beirut, Lebanon to study some fossil fishes on deposit there and to deliver a few lectures. One of the lectures was concerned with fossil mammals from American caves. After the lecture, tea and cookies were served and I had a chance to mingle with the geology students and faculty. One was Dr. Edward Carroll, an Australian geologist teaching at AUB at the time. He was a sedimentologist but had an avid interest in vertebrate fossils. He went straight to the point with, "East of here in the Jurassic limestone are many caves. Bat guano is currently being mined in one of the larger caves and the workers call me when they find bones. I received a call from them day before yesterday and they were very excited about what they say is a very strange skeleton embedded in the rock. I'm going tomorrow, and if you'd like to go...."

"I surely would, " I exclaimed. "Besides the fossils, it would give me a chance to see more of Lebanon than just Beirut."

When the reception was over, Carroll took me to the basement to show me the bones already recovered from the cave. It was an expected assortment of bones of antelope and small carnivores, plus a few relatively recent human bones. Nevertheless, I was looking forward to getting outside the city and seeing some geology.

Early the next morning, I was waiting in front of the Cedars Hotel a few blocks from the campus when he arrived in a Landrover. Even before we were out of the city, we began to climb, and before long we could look back down at the city and the Mediterranean from far above. Then, as we drove through a small stand of cedars, my mind wandered to the time when much of Lebanon was covered with cedar forests. When shipbuilding started, Lebanon became the lumberyard of the whole area. As a result of this early clear cutting, much of Lebanon has been a semi-desert ever since. In many places the white limestone lens stand almost on end, due to the earth's crust thrusting, and it gives the landscape an almost man-made look.

Soon enough we turned into a narrow cut in the limestone and drove a short distance down a rocky road until I could see the elevator support tower constructed over a vertical entrance to the cave. Before we were completely stopped, two men were running toward us shouting in Arabic. When they directed their enthusiasm to me, I looked at Carroll

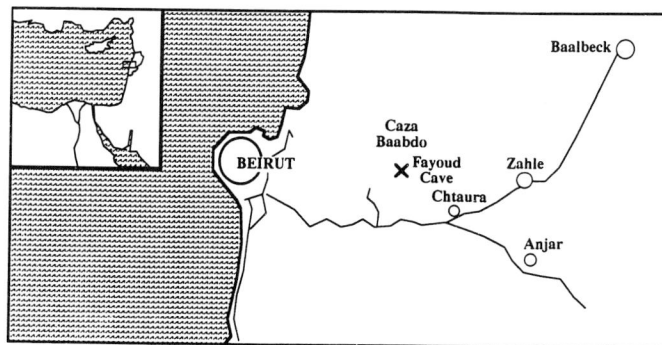

Figure 22 *Locality map of Isusu*

39

quizzically.

"I told them I had brought an expert who could tell them what they had found," he explained.

"If the skeleton is as complete as advertised, that should be a simple matter. I have been stumped, however. We call them WHATZITS," I hedged.

"Its a long way from the elevator to the old entrance and the guano quarry so I suggest we climb down the ladder used by the workmen," he said.

I was furnished a hard hat, complete with carbide lamp, and down we went. When we reached the bottom, we had to stoop for a distance. As we walked, the two men took turns explaining in Arabic while Carroll translated to me. When the guano deposit was exhausted in the area, they were cleaning up when they discovered the skeleton encapsulated in travertine. It had been covered by the guano, and that's why it had not been seen before. When we arrived, I was given plenty of room while everyone looked on expectantly. I couldn't make out much detail in the dim light, and through the rough surface of the translucent travertine coating the specimen. The skull, however, was very visible. It was quite monkey-like in that it has large eye sockets and slightly protruding front teeth. It had more inflated frontals than I have seen on any monkey, however. Even so, that was my identification and this seemed to satisfy the discoverers. We could also see that there some kind of artifacts associated with the bones. Ed arranged for the men to bring in a small electric jackhammer and break through the travertine in a wide circle around the skeleton. The travertine was not thick enough to support itself so we returned to the Landrover for the plaster and burlap. After we bandaged the block and loaded it into the Landrover, Ed gave them what he said was a generous tip, but I added an American twenty dollar bill, and they beamed.

Figure 23 *Remains of Isusu*

40

As soon as we left the cave site, I confessed to Ed that I was confused about the specimen. " It's so monkey-like I suppose it could have been a pet. That could account for the artifacts. Someone loved their pet and placed it in the cave with some offerings. Not convincing? I know! Besides the proportions are more hominoid than monkey. In any case, I hope your preparator has access to grinders, polishers, and an airscribe. It would take months to remove the travertine carefully from the skeleton by hand.

"We don't have an airscribe OR a preparator. I'm the whole show and I haven't the time or the know-how to tackle this job. I can arrange to have it shipped to Texas if you will fill out a loan form when we get back to AUB. There's no interest in the collections here so you might even be able to keep the specimen if you trade something useful in the teaching of geology. A microscope would surely do. I would like to participate in the description of the little beast, however."

"No problem. I'd enjoy co-authoring with you, and you could add a lot about the occurrence," I answered.

When we returned to the beautiful campus by the sea, we went straight to the shop and Ed had a man crate the block of travertine. He did a great job and I gave him my last twenty dollar bill. It's such a hassle to arrange transfer of a parcel from ship to truck that I had the crate addressed to the director of the Houston Museum. He's a friend and I knew he wouldn't mind accepting the specimen. So, three months later, when he called that it was there, I checked out a university carryall and took off. All the way to Houston I pondered all sorts of creatures it might be.

Even after a five hour drive home, as soon as I arrived at the university and got the crate open, I ground part of the travertine surface flat and then

Figure 24 *Isusu's sword.*

41

polished it. This allowed me to see the bones fairly well. I used an airscribe in an attempt to remove the travertine from the bone, with disastrous results. The bone is so much softer than the stone that it simply disappears when one breaks through. I decided to stick with the procedure of improving the optics of the travertine and leaving the bones in place. I therefore removed the travertine down to a half inch of the skeleton, and then polished the surface so well that I could see and measure the bones. Even more amazing than a thirty inch tall monkey-like hominoid was the fact that it apparently had wings like those of a bat. The artifacts associated proved to be a sword, still holstered and a copper-clad shield. I was almost embarrassed when I sent Ed the photos and drawings of what I'd found. If I had not been shocked by fossils of amazing creatures before, it would have been even more difficult. He showed the pictures around AUB and got only one response. Dr. Mohammed Mocmon, professor of ancient history, sent me the following comments.

"Dr. Carroll showed to me the drawings of the incredible creature you and he found here in Lebanon. It seems to fit most closely descriptions of a character usually thought to be mythical. It was known to the ancient Mesopotamians as *Pazuzu*. Ancient Assyrians speak of *Isusu* and I suspect the two are the same. Writings differ on the activities of this little demon. He has been portrayed as a bearer of disease, while others have said that he actually fought the bearers of disease, and that accounts for his sightings when there was an epidemic. Still others depict him simply as a vandal and trickster with his worst acts being puncturing water bags with his sword. The size of your specimen, the sword and power of flight all seems to fit this character. I find no mention of *Isusu/Pazuzu* after the old kingdoms of

Figure 25 *Isusu's shield.*

Mesopotamia and Assyria fell. If I had to guess at the age of the fossil, I'd say between 1000 and 500 B.C."

A radiocarbon test was run on a piece of antelope bone encased in the same layer of travertine. It produced a date of 2500 B.P. (before present) plus/minus 250. This translates to between 750 B.C. and 250 B.C. Radiocarbon dates run on bone, especially decalcified cave bone, tend to run a little young, but this one certainly fits Dr. Mocmon's guesstimate closely. The specimen has now been studied enough to present the following description.

Primopteryx carrolli, new genus and species
Fig. 23

Type specimen: LU 61278; Complete skeleton.

Diagnosis: Stood about 26 inches tall; eyes very large for skull size; teeth protruding slightly giving the face a rather monkey-like appearance although brain size is more hominoid; in addition to rather normal arms, the creature has wings like those of bats.

Etymology: *Prim (Primate) + pteryx (winged)= Winged Primate* + carrolli. Named for Edward Carroll whose untimely death precluded his completing his work.

Type locality: Fayoud Cavern 30 kilometers east of Beirut in the Caza Baabd area. (*Fig. 22*)

Description: The creature stood about 30 inches tall. Its skull is monkey-like although brain size and skeletal proportions are more hominoid. In addition to its rather normal arms and legs, it has a set of wings, not unlike those of bats. Thoracic vertebrae numbers 2 through 7 have neural spines forming a keel like the sternum of birds. Some sort of pushing muscles must have been attached here that aided flat muscles attached to the ribs in flight. The thigh bone (femur) is very short relative to the lower leg (tibia). This usually suggests fast running but this seems unlikely for a flying beast. Perhaps it gives thrust for leaping into the air for takeoff. The monkey appearance comes from the large eyes but this may be related to night and/or cave vision.

Discussion: The sword (Fig. 24) could be for things other than fighting, but I would think one would not carry a burdensome shield (Fig. 25) unless there was need. Was it to protect from arrows of humans or were there similar creatures with which to war? One view was that *Isusu* fought with the demons of disease. This is an important point, for if there were many such creatures, there is no firm evidence that this is indeed *Isusu*. The question will have to await future discoveries. Until that time, however, I think the most parsimonious view is that this is *Isusu/Pazuzu* of the Assyrian/Mesopotamian cultures. The significance of the images of vultures on the shield and sword is unknown. It could be a totem or it could merely be to invoke fear. The shields of many warlike men picture skulls and other symbols of death to rattle the enemy. The shield appears to have been carved of wood and then clad with hammered copper. The sword is of bronze. The handle is silica, perhaps volcanic glass.

There is no direct evidence concerning how the creature died. The vertical opening through which we entered may not have been the original entrance. We found what had been another vertical entrance nearby that had been blocked by a ceiling collapse. It's possible that *Isusu* was in the cave when it was closed and the new entrance opened much later. It is equally possible that *Isusu* was laid to rest with his weapons by a colleague after dying from wounds or disease. It seems unlikely that he would have kept his shield with him if he were trapped. Pollen analysis of the sediments directly beneath the travertine was extremely high in cedar pollen, suggesting the cedar forests were intact at the time.

JO BO (JOY BOY)

Jmust admit that, as a paleontologist, I was always a grandstander. My students and I loved to think up a really great research problem to solve and then spend a great deal of effort to pull it off. Tough research problems offer many defeats but when one hits, it holds a special feeling. On Friday afternoons, my graduate students and colleagues from Geology, Biology, and Anthropology would meet at a pub near the University to discuss new facts and technologies and brainstorm their possible use in the solving of old problems and developing new and exciting questions to pose. One day we discussed the Caribbean and what kind of BIG questions might be solved in that beautiful space (in the winter, of course).

We all knew the fauna of the West Indies seems to be part North American and part South American. There is also an idea that New World Fruit bats had their origins on the islands. Finding some fossils of early mammalian immigrants to the West Indies would indeed be interesting. The next step would be to identify a specific island that: (1) has outcroppings of deposits of Mio-Pliocene age which would be available to the likes of us, and (2) offered projects important enough to furnish some funding. The sequence of discussion, started as usual, with logistics. Who speaks English? Jamaica! Who has an active Geological Survey to aid our endeavor? Jamaica! Ok! Lets see what we can

find out about the geology and paleontology of Jamaica before next Friday. I managed to steal a few hours that next week to spend in the library and discovered that only three fossil monkeys had been found in all of the West Indies. One was from Cuba and that was off limits. The other two were from the Dominican Republic and Jamaica. Spanish is spoken in the Dominican Republic and English in Jamaica so we opted for the latter. The Jamaican specimen was a lower jaw fragment of a small monkey and was either Pleistocene or Recent in age. Certainly, there were no monkeys on the islands when Columbus landed. This important fossil had been found in Long Mile Cave near the village of Winsor in 1922.

"Now that sounds interesting. If we could find enough of a monkey from the mainland that reached the West Indies and could date it properly and identify its area of origin. . . Central or South America. . . splash!!"

I had met an Englishman by the name of Alan Fincham at a Florida meeting who taught at the University of the West Indies in Jamaica but that was several years ago. I found and contacted Fincham, who now lives in the States and he knew the cave. He referred me to Dr. Buddy Steiniger, Geologist with the University of the West Indes, saying "Buddy always had a group of enthusiastic spelunkers he recruited from the student body. He and/or his students have been in almost all of the caves on the island."

Instead of dragging out the procedure by trying to exchange several letters, my wife and I decided just to take off and go there in person. We landed in Montego Bay, rented a small car, got a good firm

Figure 26 *JoBo's burial drum.*

tooth lock on our lips, and started off on the wrong side of the road. Dr. Steiniger's office was in Kingston at the other end of the island so we planned a route that would show us as much of the terrain as possible while getting there. Dr. Steiniger was very hospitable and put us in touch with several local spelunkers. When interviewing each, we tried to evaluate caves' potential for producing fossil bones from their descriptions. When we interviewed one young spelunker, Laton Thomas, he said that he had something he'd like to show us. His story went something like this:

"My girl friend, Vernetta, and I decided to investigate a small cave her uncle told her about. My friends told me that they knew of no caves in that area so I decided I would get the jump on them. The small cave turned out to be in sandstone, instead of limestone, and only penetrated the hill about fifty feet. It has a sandy floor and there is no place one can stand upright. We dug a hole about 18" deep in the floor at the rear of the small cave and all we found was a cigar wrapper. . . Not very impressive.

"We were sitting at the entrance just looking out over the beautiful valley. Vernetta was sitting next to a four foot sandstone boulder that had fallen from the overhang. She scratched in the sand by the boulder and asked asked me, "What's this?"

The edge of a large wooden bowl was sticking out from under the boulder. Either the rock had fallen from above onto some sort of artifact, or the boulder was placed there to conceal the bowl. If it is something of interest, I would prefer that it go to a museum rather than to be sold on the market place."

We congratulated him on his attitude and agreed to have a look. Dr. Steiniger said it would be a good idea to have Laton with us anyway, since we could happen upon a Ganja growing area and

46

would need a local to explain our presence. Laton called Vernetta and when we picked her up, my wife took an instant liking to the lovely young lady. All the while we drove they chatted and giggled like they had known each other all their lives. After stopping at a sand pit and a couple road cuts to look for fossils, we arrived as a lovely resort-type place called Milk River and stopped for lunch. The resort is there because of hot springs. People have been using the naturally hot water therapeutically for over 200 years. After a very tasty and healthful lunch, our young guide introduced us to the lady who owned the establishment. He told us during lunch that she was rather superstitious. Sure enough, when she discovered that we were paleontologists (many people equate us with archaeologists), she asked if we were familiar with JoBo. Not having heard of JoBo before, she proceeded to tell us a little more than we wanted to know.

Figure 27 *Close-up of JoBo skull.*

It seems JoBo is a sort of spirit that came to the Americas from Africa with the slaves. All of his efforts went to trying to keep these enslaved people's spirits up through music, singing, and dancing. No one could resist the rhythm of his drum beat. Everyone would dance and sing as long as he played, or they dropped. Afterwards, their problems seemed much less important. There may have been more than one JoBo, however, because he has been known for generations throughout the Islands. I like the concept that JoBo gives hope to the oppressed and promotes joy even when one is blue.

When she had our undivided attention she added that she often heard a Jobo singing and playing his drum higher up the hill and it always set her to dancing.

We reserved a cabin for the evening and pressed on to the sandstone cave. When we reached the

47

spot, we had to climb quite a way but the scenery was such that it alone was well worth it. When we arrived, Laton swept some loose sand from the edge of a wooden pot sticking out from under the large rock. He started to dig but then decided it would be prudent to remove the rock first. We dug some of the sand from the downhill side and then with the help of a eight foot limb, pried the boulder far enough to start it rolling down the hill. After that, the digging was simple and we had the complete circle of the rim of the vessel exposed in no time. Laton and I dug with our hands around the outside while Juliana and Vernetta concentrated their efforts to removing the sand from within the vessel. As soon as I realized that it was palm, I wondered if it was indeed an artifact. Palm centers rot more rapidly than the outside, often leaving a wooden sleeve. Natural origin soon was not a question, however for Vernetta encountered a human skull. At that moment we heard in the distance a man singing joyously to the beat of a drum.

"Radio?" I inquired quizzically, but Laton said, wide-eyed, "Not around here!"

I asked the girls not to remove any more sand from within until we had the vessel excavated and evaluated. To shorten the story let me just say that the vessel proved to be a large palmwood drum that had served as a casket for the semi-articulated bones of a tall male. Wear marks of leather thongs holding the skins that had covered each end were evident (Fig. 26). Every single one of the individual's teeth were gold (Fig. 27). With that realization, Laton seemed to become very nervous.

"What's the problem?" I asked.

"The gold teeth and the drum burial suggest that this is a JoBo," he responded.

Vernetta cutely placing her hands on her hips said to Laton, "So, what's the problem? JoBo is a friendly spirit, right?"

"I guess so," Laton replied, "but a spirit is a spirit."

We took the burial drum back to the Geological survey, then to the museum and the university. Everyone we showed it to felt it was a JoBo. Some call it a Joy Boy and I'm not sure if Joy Boy was derived from JoBo, or the other way around. I suspect JoBo was the original name as Joy Boy is clearly English and the legend occurs on French and Spanish-speaking islands, as well. In any case, the two names seem to be interchangeable. Whether JoBo, or Joy Boys, are indeed spirits, or just a group of troubadours following tradition, I could not find out. It seems that having all their teeth replaced with gold is going rather far for tradition, however. Most Jamaicans I asked were adamant that JoBo are friendly spirits dedicated to making people happier.

There is nothing so unusual about the skeleton that removes it from the range of variation of modern humans. He was tall, perhaps 6'6", with a large but thin skull. The full set of gold teeth is unusual but possible for anyone. The one thing that is impossible to evaluate is the feelings one gets when close to the specimen. Even people who don't know the legend tend to sing, or hum, and break into a shuffle or tap their feet when in the proximity. As one who belittles worries, I sincerely hope this is not the last of the JoBo.

KOKOPELLI

n 1964, Dr. Claude Albritton, the graduate dean, called me to his office and told me that Mr. Marvin Tong, Director of the Museum of the Great Plains in Oklahoma, had made a proposal. The dam for Lake Amsted on the Rio Grande between Texas and Mexico was under construction. The University of Texas salvage archeologists were doing an antiquities survey within the lake basin on the Texas side, but nothing was being done on the Mexican side. Tong's proposal was for the Museum of the Great Plains to furnish an archaeologist, one Frank Leonardy, and our university to furnish a vertebrate paleontologist, me, and we would do the survey of the Mexican side together. Was I interested?

"Why not?" was my immediate response.

By the time we were ready to leave, both Tong and the Dean decided to join the expedition and the Dean's teenage son, Claude Jr., wanted to go as well. So, there were five of us in the field vehicle plus equipment. When we got to Villa Cuna, Mexico, we took on two local men as guides and then we were really packed. The Mexican officials in Villa Cuna furnished us with a map and a key that was said to open any gate along the road for seventy five miles, and off we went. The roads marked on the map turned out to be goat trails and we often had to fill in gullies across them by hand. The next afternoon found us only thirty miles west of where we started. We had destroyed two of our

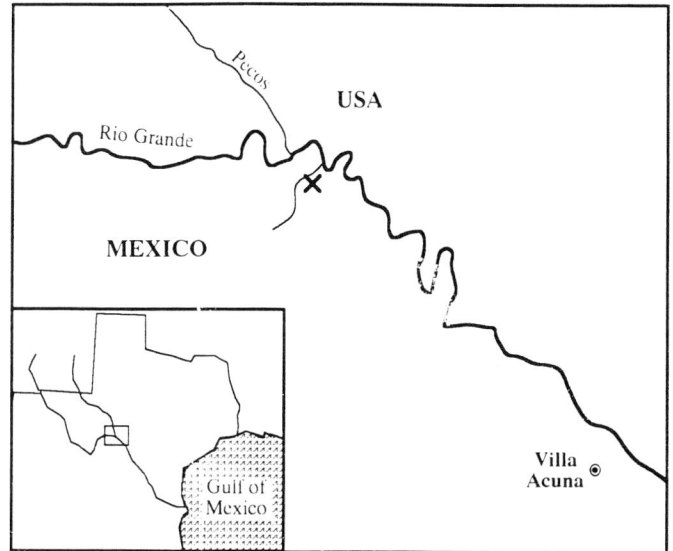

Figure 28 *Location of flooded Kokopelli tomb.*

four spare tires, which worried me quite a bit. By late evening we encountered our third gate and the key would not fit. We were less than forty miles out and felt that the lock had been changed by mistake. Therefore, feeling within our rights, we took the gate off its hinges and swung it on its chain, passed through, put it back, and continued on. Soon enough, we came to a beautiful hacienda but the people waiting there were not pleased to see us. In fact since the boss was not there, they would not allow us to get out of the truck. It was hours later and already dark when a truck full of herders arrived with the boss driving. Suspecting that we had been losing something through our translators, I rushed to the "boss" and started to explain in English. He held up his hand and told us to follow

51

one of the men and then he disappeared into the big house. We were led to a guest house and seated around a large hand carved dining table with the head seat left vacant, obviously for the boss. After a bit the boss, in the form of one Rico Escobar appeared; bathed, clean shaven, and wearing a white sport coat. He sat at the head of the table, turned to me, and said "Now!"

It was very clear that we were not supposed to be there but after we explainined what we were doing, he was pleased. It turned out that he had a degree from Louisiana State University. He turned the guest house over to us and gave us a guide. The next morning we visited several Indian pictograph sites and photographed a few. I hated to think about these examples of ancient art being covered by the lake waters.

One flute-playing character was depicted often. Frank explained, "It probably was a fellow known to the Hopi, Zuni, and Navajos as *Kokopelli*. Petroglyphs and pictographs of the near-deity are known from Utah to Mexico. Sometimes he's pictured with horns and cloven hooves, but sometime he isn't. He always plays a flute, and often has a rather large penis. This, no doubt, is why the modern tribes consider him a symbol of fertility."

"Sounds like our old friend, *Pan*," young Claude added.

Rico said that he had saved the largest and most impressive rock shelter until tomorrow because he wanted to revisit it himself, and the next day being Sunday, we would all go together.

We took the same big truck that was used to deliver and retrieve the workers, and I found it great fun. The ride was very rough, but we could hang onto the sideboards and look out over the cab. Rico would point out wildlife and interesting plants. He was actually quite a naturalist. When we arrived at a great cliff, we drove right up to the

Figure 29 *Entrance to Kokopelli burial cave.*

52

edge. We then climbed down a path and entered a huge rock shelter, measuring about one hundred feet wide and and extending sixty feet back into the limestone. The walls and ceiling were covered with pictographs of red, yellow, black, and some white. The floor was dusty and there was a six foot diameter hole dug in the middle. Rico told us that when he was a young boy he dug the hole looking for arrowheads but it proved too much effort for the reward. Exposed in the walls of his excavation we could see woven grass mats and sandals, as well as shards of pottery. Rico went here and there pointing to pictures of our friend *Kokopelli*. It was he who pointed out that the older looking pictures were the ones that portrayed the figure with horns and cloven hooves.

"Interesting," I thought.

As it was Claude Jr. and I who seemed the most interested in *Kokopelli*, Rico took us aside and said that he knew where the best petroglyph of the character was.

"Its not far away, and if the others want to work here, we can go there," he said.

"Lets go!"

We drove right to the cliffs overlooking the Rio Grande. We climbed down a distance and there was a small opening that reminded me of many tiny tombs dug by the common people near the Valley of the Kings in Egypt. We stooped over and entered. It had the feel of a tomb, as well. There in the sand floor was a flat rock about two feet in diameter with painted petroglyphs on its surface. There was one very nice picture of Kokopelli wearing a red gown and with a yellow flute. Curiously, the flute could be seen through his body and one had the feeling that it was a picture of an ascension (Fig. 31). Other painted petroglyphs depicted catfish, a rabbit, a turtle, targets, deer, mountain sheep, and what appeared to be boats. It

Figure 30 *Kokopelli remains.*

53

There were more mountain sheep than anything else.

"Rico," I said, "this seems a most appropriate place for such a stone, but as you know it will go under the lake unless fishermen docking their boats here before the lake fills take it home as a curiosity. How would you feel about our collecting the stone? This way, it can at least be appreciated and perhaps wind up in a museum."

He agreed, although I could tell it saddened him. We returned to the rock shelter a short distance away to get help. When we tried to pry the "flat rock" out of the floor, however, we discovered it was the top of a cylinder, not a flat rock, and weighed several hundred pounds. It was made of lightly fired adobe rather than rock, and had petroglyphs on all surfaces.

"Still want to collect it?" Juan teased.

When I said, "By all means," everyone groaned. It took lots of grunts and groans getting the several hundred pound "rock" the 60 feet up the steep hill and into the truck. Back at the hacienda I was almost outvoted as to hauling that much weight back in our overloaded trailer. Nevertheless, I prevailed.

When we returned to Dallas, I offered the piece to Frank, but he declined. Frank was interested in much earlier cultures, and the preparation would be time consuming. I don't know why the job appealed to me so much, but I know it had something to do with the drawing of Kokopelli on top. When I cleaned the big cylinder I realized that the petroglyph on the sides meant that the adobe was not merely dumped into a cylindrical hole. It was probably stuccoed onto something and after it was hardened, the petroglyphs (Figs. 31, 32) were added before it was buried. I decided to take it to a friend at the medical school who could x-ray the block. My hunch was right. This was a basket burial and it contained a complete skeleton. Some southwestern American Indians placed their dead in shelters or caves and, after the flesh had more or less decayed, they would gather the bones, put them in a large basket and bury them. A new twist was added here, however. The basket was stuccoed on the outside for strength and then it was filled with adobe. Only then was the solid "rock" casket decorated and buried.

"This must have been SOMEBODY," I thought.

I stabilized the adobe by saturating it with Alvar and went at it with an airscribe (a small pneumatic chisel). Immediately, I encountered the basket. Guided by the X-ray, I cut through the basket in front of the skeleton and continued my excavation. First I uncovered an upper arm bone, then the straight but flaring flute lying diagonally across the individual's chest. Each bone I encountered I chiseled in relief but many could not be exposed except to the detriment of others. At the end of the exceptionally short tibia (lower leg bone) were foot bones like those of an artiodactyl (cloven hoofed animal). After that, I had to go for the skull. Before getting there, I encountered long braids of black and gray hair. I followed one of these directly to the skull. The features of this face were very fine, almost androgynous. I can't say I expected it, but I was not surprised when I found the horns. A pair of horns slightly twirled like those of a young mountain sheep ram extended from the frontals.

I had only learned about Kokopelli a couple of weeks before and now to stumble on his remains in such an out of the way place in Mexico made the hair on my neck stand up. I put the airscribe down and wondered what to do. I could see the horned skull, the telltale cloven hooves, and the flute.

Figure 31 *Petroglyphs on burial basket; sides.*

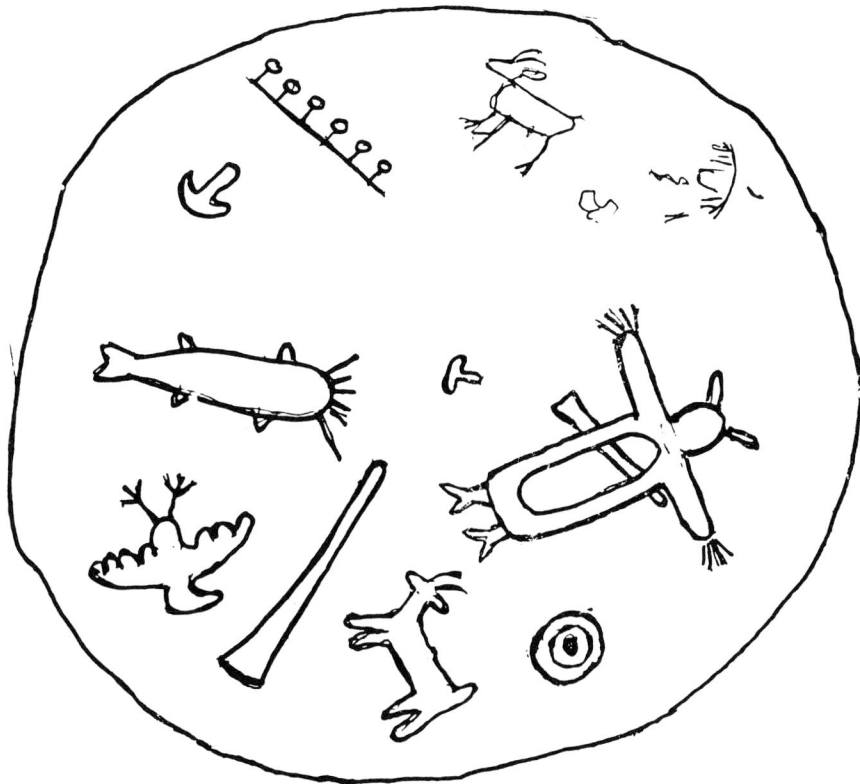

Figure 32 *Petroglyphs on burial baskets; top.*

"I think I'll leave the rest as it was meant to be. Maybe even drive back down to Mexico and return it to its tomb. . . . Doesn't make sense, however. If I do, when the lake is finished, it will either be lost to the lake waters or will be discovered by those who would not appreciate it. And besides, Kokopelli might enjoy the company of the illustrious group of mythical creatures stored here."

I felt humbled by the mere presence of this burial. After all, it probably is the individual adored by Indians and artists from Utah to Mexico for up to twenty centuries.

Homovis albrittoni, new genus and species
Fig. 30

Diagnosis: Not unlike the skeleton of modern man except for the feet and horns of a mountain sheep.

Type locality: State of Coahuila, Mexico (Fig. 28) in a small cave facing a little canyon off the Rio Grande just a few hundred yards downstream from where the Pecos River enters the Rio Grande from the Texas side.

Etymology: Homo (man) + Ovis (sheep) *albrittoni* for Dr. Claude Albritton, the most scholarly geologist I've ever known.

Discussion: According to the number of petroglyths and pictographs of Kokopelli that occur throughout the southwestern U.S. and northern Mexico and the time span of several hundred years, he would have to be considered a major deity. Many of the images were executed by Anasazi, Hokokam, Mongollon, and other Basket Weaver artists beyond the memory of modern Pueblo tribes (Navajo, Zuni, Hopi, etc.). I feel that those pictographs that depict *Kokopelli* with horns and cloven hooves are the earlier drawings and when the deity was picked up by the later tribes, they pictured him with horns but with normal human feet. I suspect the horns are part of a head dress and these pictures are of men dressed like *Kokopelli*, Kachina-like.

The bones are not in complete articulation. The feet are, as are the hands, but the limb bones are only loosely associated. This is similar to other early Indian basket-burials— the exception being that the basket is encapsulated in adobe. No doubt the body was allowed to at least partially deteriorate before the bones were gathered and buried with such pomp.

The flute is not unlike that used by Aztecs of southern Mexico. It has a flare or bell at the distal end (Fig. 30) whereas the Navajo flutes I've seen are the same diameter all the way down. The flute is made of wood and then native copper was tooled over it. The copper can be traced to the Great Lakes area and probably arrived in the southwest as a trade item.

A radiocarbon date on some of the removed basket material produced a date of A.D. 1300 plus or minus 150 years before present, translating to A.D. 1150 to 1450. The Anasazi, or Ancient People, disappeared during this period making *Kokopelli* one more mythical creature that apparently died when the culture that believed in him ended.

In the early 1970s, the Society of Vertebrate Paleontology held its annual meeting in Toronto. I checked into the official hotel mid-afternoon the day before the meetings were to start, and strolled into the hotel bar. There I saw a colleague, one Dr. Robert McDonald, a specialist in fossil birds.

"Hey Bob, what exciting stuff you been digging up?" I exclaimed.

"I've really had tough duty," he replied, "I've been collecting sub-Recent bird remains in Hawaii. Most of them occur in old beach dune deposits and in solution tubes in the volcanic rock. As you know, birds often evolve flightless forms on islands where there are no reptile or mammal predators. Hawaii was no exception. I've discovered a whole host of flightless forms. I even found a flightless owl with long running legs. Of course, they all became extinct soon after the arrival of man about 4,000 years ago."

"A stilt-legged owl! Wow! I don't suppose you came across any rodents?" I inquired.

"No rodents on the islands before sailing ships arrived in the l6th Century. I did see an interesting rodent occurrence, however. While looking for solution tubes, I came across a boulder that was riddled with small mini-caves. All were plugged with clay and protruding from the clay I sometimes saw bones of rats. I suspect they were placed there by birds. I didn't collect any as they could only be the common roof rat."

About that time, other "bone men" began filing in and we both saw other friends to visit with. I filed his comments under "interesting."

Several years later I dropped by to visit with a grand lady, Jane Albritton, widow of my mentor, Dr. Claude Albritton. I wanted to tell her that I'd named one of my creatures after Claude. When I showed her the photographs of *Kokopelli*, her husband's namesake, she told me that I should go collect some remains of *Menehune*. Jane grew up in Hawaii and she unfurled the following story:

"As a young girl I went horseback riding a lot. One time a group of us rode down to Helina Pali, a cliff south of the Kilauea Caldera. Our guide was Johnny Maikaimoku. Suddenly the horses stopped and refused to move forward. Johnny placed his index finger over his lips and cupped the other hand behind his ear. He then motioned us to turn around and go back down the path. After we had ridden a short distance, he dismounted and motioned for us to do the same. We all sat down on the rocks holding our horses' reins. He explained in a loud whisper, 'I heard the humming of the *Menehune*. I suspect they were about to cross the trail and the horses will not get in their way.'

"Several others said that they too had heard the humming, but just thought it was the wind in the rocks.

"Johnny told us, 'The Menehune are tiny people, about six or seven inches tall. They are very powerful, however, and neither men nor horses will cross them. It will be all right to pass shortly.'

"Several of the riders laughed rudely to express

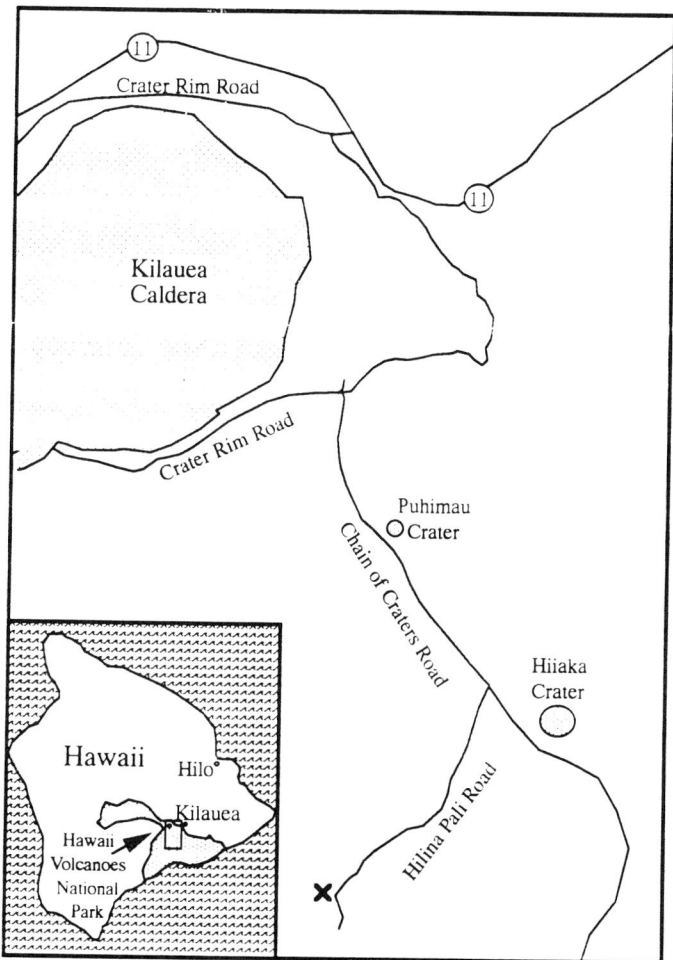

Figure 33 *Menehune locality.*

their skepticism. The story sounded rather far fetched to me too, but I liked Johnny and certainly would never be rude to him. In about fifteen minutes we remounted and passed the place on the trail without event. The next day he was at the house early, saying that he would like to prove the existence of the *Menehune* to me if I was up for a long ride. It was indeed a long ride from where we unloaded the horses. Finally he dismounted and pointed to a boulder. The boulder was a dark red in color. Here and there was a tiny cave full of softer deposits, also of a reddish color. He pointed to small bones protruding from these cave fillings.

""'Johnny, those are just bones of field mice.' I said. He produced a pocket knife and dug into two or three of the tiny caves exposing skulls that did indeed look exactly like human skulls, except for their small size."

Needless to say, I was flashing back to my conversation with Bob McDonald. The next day I visited the university library, checked out a topographic map of the Big Island, and returned to Jane's home. She showed me the area where she had seen the unusual boulder and I had a Xerox of the map made. I sent a copy to McDonald, asking him to mark the place where he saw the "rat bones." When he returned my map I could see that it was not too far from the area where Jane had her *Menehune* experience.

My wife had long been wanting to visit Carolyn Davis, a friend living in Hawaii, so there was no problem justifying a trip. When we arrived, I showed Carolyn the map and she told us that there was a road through the area now. "In fact there is even a parking lot for people wanting to photograph the volcano."

So, armed with a small awl and the map, we took off in Carolyn's small red car, which was made even redder by rust. It ran well, however, and

Figure 34 *Menehune Mausoleum Rock*

it didn't take her long to pull into the parking lot. The problem was not so much finding the cave-riddled stones but finding one close enough to the car that the girls and I could lift. When I did choose one, I used the awl to excavate the tiny caves to see if they were as advertised. They were, and we collected the boulder, which sank Carolyn's tiny hatchback to the springs.

After returning to the university and preparing each small cave entrance to put the bones in relief, I sent Dr. McDonald some photographs with a note saying, "Here're your rats."

Return mail was just a Smithsonian Institution post card saying, "Looks like a *Homo slaughteri* to me."

Menehune albrittoni, new genus and species
Fig. 34

Type specimens: Fourteen small skulls with associated vertebrae and long bones.

Diagnosis: Like skeletons of *Homo sapiens* except for their tiny size (about 100 millimeters); fibula fused with the tibia (lower leg bones) at both ends which no doubt led Dr. McDonald to the field identification of some of the bones as those of rodents.

Locality: The crater of the volcano Kilauea is circled by Crater Rim Drive; South from this road on Chain of Craters Road to Hilina Pali Road (Fig. 31).

Etymology: *Menehune* after the native legend and *albrittoni* in honor of Jane Albritton, whose story was necessary to send me collecting.

Discussion: The Menehune are said to be very industrious and work the whole night through on various projects from moving water around for irrigation to building themselves swimming pools. They often underestimate the number of *Menehune* a job will take however, and if they don't complete a project before dawn, they abandon it and began a new project the next night. The legends of *Menehune* predate the coming of Europeans but to my knowledge these are the first remains of these tiniest of hominoids reported.

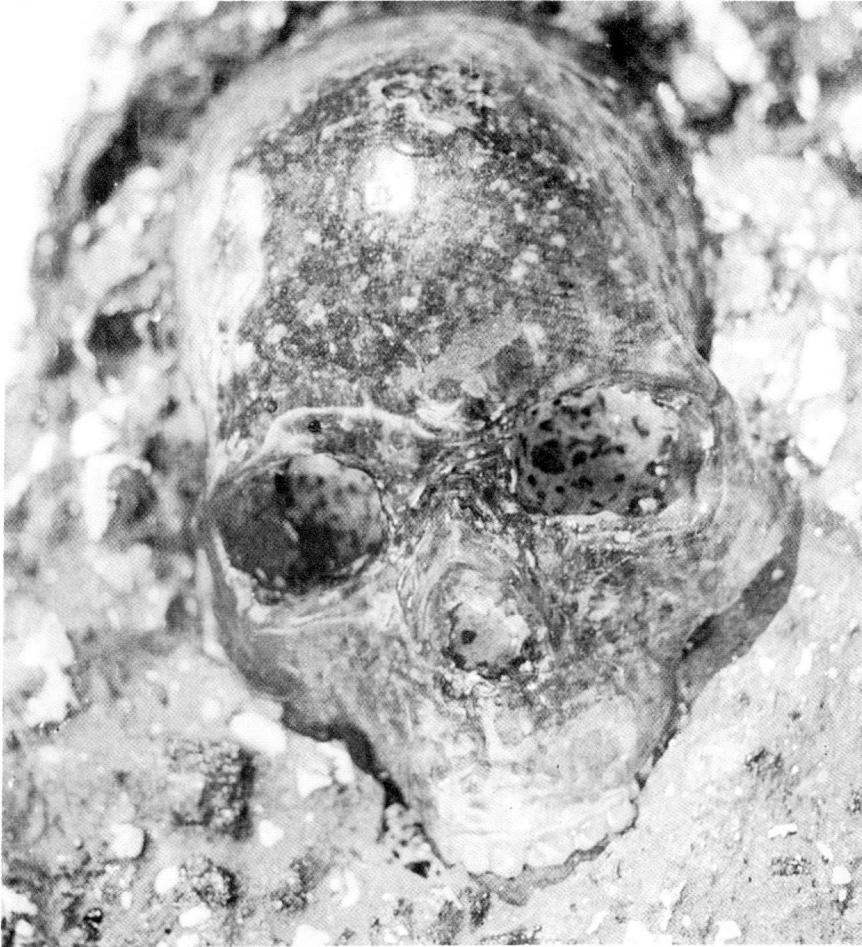

Figure 35 *Transparent skull of El Nahual* .

64

EL NAHUAL

My wife, Juliana, is director of an Artist in Residence program housed in an old Cotton Gin, not far from the University. I enjoy the presence of creative people, so I visit the residency often. When the famous Mexican painter, Antonio Ramirez was in residence, we became good friends. He was as interested in my fringe hominoids as I was in his most interesting painting style. One day shortly before he was leaving to return to Mexico, he told me about a "magic place" in Yucatan where he believed the remains of *El Nahual* were. He said he had not mentioned it before because he had not actually seen the remains. Two relatives had told him about it, and he was certain they were telling him the truth. The story goes something like this:

"Near the small camposino village of Ichmul there's an escarpment of about twenty feet, over which a narrow waterfall flows into a very clear pool. The local people used the pool for bathing and washing clothes. These people had an unusually large number of encounters with *El Nahual*. There may be many *Nahuals* in that it's said each time there's a human birth, the baby's counterpart, or spirit double, comes into being. *Nahual* may be good or bad for humanity, according to mood, or deserts, and may appear as any animal. In its human mode, however, *Nahual* is invisible and therefore no one knows what he/she looks like. Sometimes the name is applied to a vague personage who is a sort of scape goat. He is blamed for the pregnancy of young girls, and when a wild dog would steal a chicken, it was *El Nahual* in disguise who was the culprit, and so on.

"Once, when such mischief was at its peak, a local camposino put a pan dulce (pastry) laced with poison in the fork of a tree where the children couldn't get at it. That night, strange and pitiful cries were heard from the forest and the farmer began to wonder if he had done the right thing. Sure enough, the mischief ceased but natural catastrophes of much greater proportions seemed to take over. Floods, insect hoards, and drought increased until almost everyone left the area. At the height of a three year drought, things got so bad that the waterfall stopped flowing. My uncle Roberto went to see the dry pool and in the shallow end of the pool was what appeared to be a skeleton thinly covered with algae. He had a very strange feeling in the presence of the skeleton and ran away. About a year later he returned to the pool to show it to his daughter, Celia. There was some water in the pool then but it was shallow and very clear. The skeleton was no where in sight.

"Several years later, after Uncle Roberto had died, Celia returned from her new home in Mérida to visit the area where she spent her childhood. She naturally went to the pool and there in the shallow was something that was difficult for her to describe. She said she could see no skeleton but if there were a skeleton, the face was right at, or slightly above the surface. As the tiny ripples passed over the "skull" she could make out features. Still it was invisible. She reached out and touched this invisible skull and she felt something like an electric shock. It frightened her and she, too, ran away. When trying to explain it, she usually referred to it

65

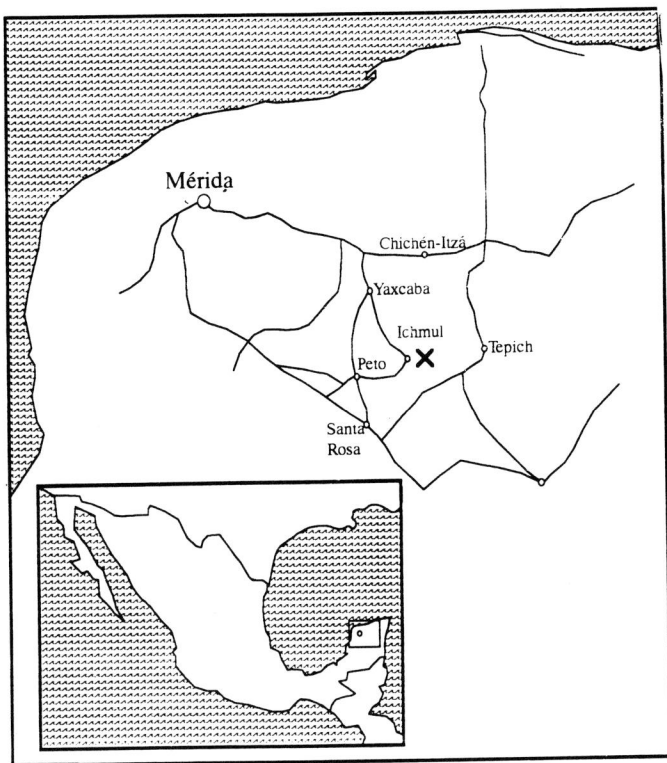
Figure 36 *El Nahual locality.*

as an 'invisible skull.'"

Antonio added, "To my knowledge, no one else has investigated this claim, but my cousin is adamant in the belief that it is the remains of *El Nahual* the farmer had poisoned."

Well, Antonio's story was certainly intriguing but even if true, how could one find and collect an invisible skull? Even so, when my wife and I decided to take a brief vacation to Isla Mujeres, I called Antonio and he and his wife, Enriqueta, met us in Mérida. Celia lived there and agreed to serve as our guide. It was nearly a mile walk through lush jungles to get to the pool and I wondered how

such a place would look during a three year drought. When we arrived, Celia pointed to the spot but explained that the water is now deeper, and after all the skull is invisible. She was almost apologetic, as if its absence reflected on her integrity. The bottom had a deep blanket of pebbles ranging in color from black, through the grays, to white. Their hues were made vivid by the clear water. I used my machete like a rake to drag it about in the area where Celia pointed and, incredibly, I dragged out an absolutely clear humerus (upper arm bone).

At the university I've seen biologists clear bones by soaking them in glycerin but they were always those of mouse-size animals and usually fetal. I've certainly never seen an adult bone cleared, in or outside the laboratory. What to do? If I continued to rake I might break something important but, denied sight, how else could I find more of the skeleton?

I remembered that when I was a student, my professor amazed me by making plaster molds of some dinosaur tracks under water. He simply sifted plaster-of-paris on the surface of the water and allowed it to sink into the track. Much to my surprise, the plaster set as if it was not in water at all. Quiet water is needed, however, as any current will disperse the powered plaster. So, Antonio and I set to building a sort of dike around the area to isolate the spot from any current in the pool. Meanwhile, Juliana and Enriqueta drove back to Mérida and borrowed two bags of plaster from an group of archaeologists from Southern Methodist University we had met earlier. The experiment was a success. Although we were not sure what we had, we could see the shape of a skull as the plaster first "rained" down over it. We tied the whole thing together with more plaster and burlap and, the next day, removed the blob. The pebble bed came with it, as the plaster had filled the spaces between the pebbles. At least we had some of the skeleton and we knew we had the skull.

Back at the university we added a much better plaster bandage over the top of the block which had originally been the bottom. Then we carefully cut away the plaster we had applied in the field. This gave us the same view Roberto and Celia had of the specimen. Without the water the bones were not totally invisible but rather clear like glass. We cleaned the block of pool pebbles with its "invisible" bones and coated them with tempera paint for study. Try as I may, I could find no difference that could distinguish the clear bones from those of a modern human being. I have discussed this phenomnon with numerous organic chemists and biologists and none has come up with a reasonable explanation as to how large bones could be "cleared" naturally. In the absence of any other explanation, and although it is bound to be controversial, I agree that the skeleton may be an example of what the local people call *El Nahual* in that they are said to be invisible when in human form. Invisibility is certainly not a feature of Homo sapiens so I feel this very unusual form should be distinguished by a new designation.

Homo ramirezi, new species
Fig. 35

Diagnosis: Skeleton indistinguishable from modern man save the curious feature of being quite clear. Stained thin-sections of pieces of the skull show typical histology of a normal bone.

Locality: Five miles by motor trail and one mile by foot almost due east of the small village of Ichmul southeast of Mérida, Yucatan, Mexico (Fig. 36).

Etymology: Named for Antonio Ramirez, friend, scholar and artist extraordinare.

Discussion: *El Nahual* is a sort of tonal, or personal spirit. Legend has it that when an Indian is born, so is his/her *Nahual*. Therefore, there must have been many *Nahuales* unless when a person dies, the *Nahual* passes onto a newborn and begins the cycle over. In any case, there must have been billions and it is curious that the remains of so few have been found. Its said that *Nahual* may take on the shape of any animal but no one knows what he looks like in his human mode, due to his invisibility. I see no possible utility for clear bones unless the blood and flesh also were clear also, making the creature nearly invisible. The invisible mode being manifest in death suggests that visibility was an effort, not invisibility. Any person, or creature, blamed for bad luck usually is responsible for a small fraction of the allegations. On the other hand, I doubt that anyone given the ability to become invisible, could resist an occasional bit of mischief. *El Nahual* can be good for someone, or bad, according to his mood or the person's deserts. It's said that when one kills a *Nahual* while it is an animal, its human counterpart also becomes sick and dies.

When one looks at our skull they cannot help but think of the crystal skulls found at some Aztec sites. They are said to be carved from large crystals and, indeed, most I've of them I've seen pictured are very stylized. I have heard of two, however, that are so realistic that, if painted, would pass for an actual skull. I'd like to examine one of these to see if it's possible that they are indeed skulls of *Nahuales*. Even if ours is the only one, it seems likely that the crystal carvings represent the skulls of *Nahuales*. Therefore some Aztecs must have seen such a skull as this. Just what *Nahual* is is difficult to get a handle on. Some think of it as a sort of guardian spirit. Some think of it as a mean, mischievous prankster.

NEPTUNOIDES

ack in the sixties, on Tuesday nights, my wife usually had dinner out with her friend, Helen, and took in a movie. I spent a couple hours with my friend, Wayne, at the Rose Bar and Grill discussing the week, our work, and world affairs. We were older than most of the patrons and we usually sat at the end of the bar where there were only three stools— out of the way, you might say. This night, there was a gentleman slightly older than ourselves on the other stool but he didn't join in. After one beer, Wayne gulped his last swallow, pulled on his sweater and said he had to meet a client at his studio. As I sat silent, the gentleman sitting next to me spoke for the first time.

"So you're a paleontologist?" he inquired.

"Why, yes. How did you know?" I replied.

"I didn't mean to eavesdrop, but. . . ." he said, shrugging his shoulders.

The barkeep approached me, pointing to my empty glass. "No more for me, thanks," I said. "Heading for the barn,"

The gentleman next to me, speaking anxiously, said, "Give him one on me."

He turned on his stool, full face, and said he didn't want to inconvenience me but he had something to tell of great importance. He spoke with a thick German accent and it was clear that he was very well educated.

"My name is Wilhelm Voss," he said, extend-ing his hand. "Have you ever been to the Middle East?"

"Many times. I've done a lot of work in Egypt."

"Do you know the area around Al Alamayn?"

"Quite well. In fact, I'll be in that area this coming January."

This seemed to please him and he said, "Now I know that you're the one I must tell my story to."

"Shoot," I said. "Always ready for a good story."

"It was 1943 and I was in Greece with the German army. I was a captain and attache to Colonel Klaus Meyer. Meyer was director of a famous museum before the war and was placed in charge of collecting art and antiquities in occupied countries for the new international museum to be built in Germany after we won the war. There was a German soldier whose hobby was archaeology and he spent his spare time collecting artifacts. It seems that it was this activity that brought him to pry up some floor stones of the Greek Temple of Posedion near Sounion where he was stationed. Do you know the temple?"

"I've been there a couple times," I replied. "It's a beautiful place."

"Well," he continued, "He presented himself at Meyer's office in Athens and told of seeing a skeleton dressed in armor under the floor. That was enough for Meyer. He called me in and told me to take the soldier with a truck and crew to Sounion and excavate the whatever.

"When we arrived at Posedion we removed several of the smooth limestone floor stones and sure enough, there were parts of a skeleton and a bronze breast plate protruding from a bed of cemented shell hash. The bones seemed fossilized

Figure 37 *Odyssey of Neptunoides.*

and I wondered how they got into the rock, for surely they couldn't be more than a couple thousand years old. In any case, we collected the specimen and brought it to Meyer's office. He was very pleased and told me to have it crated and shipped to the Libian port of Bengasi in care of Field Marshal Rommel. Only then did he tell me that we were to accompany Rommel on his assault on Egypt. It seems that Meyer wanted to be first to pick and choose from the Egyptian antiquities for his precious museum.

"Well, I followed instructions and a few weeks later in Bengasi, Meyer ordered me to load the crate on our truck and make ready to join the caravan to Cairo. I did so, but as you know, we never made Cairo. Such massive resistance from the British and their allies was met at Al Alameyn that Rommel's forces were thrown into retreat. With the battle going badly, our truck became part of a retreating caravan of trucks and other military vehicles. Meyer told us to watch for a road leading south. When one appeared, we stopped, and Meyer requisitioned a truck load of soldiers and we took the road south. We soon reached a vast depression I later found out was the Qattarah Depression. There was a steep road down the escarpment and Meyer walked down, ordering us to wait at the top. He disappeared and it seemed like an eternity before he came into view again. Remember we were twenty miles or so off the main road and presumably the Allies were advancing. Meyer directed us to drive down. He had found a narrow but deep ravine just east of the road that had very steep walls of loose sand and rock. We backed as close as we dared and dumped the crate into the ravine. We then created a slide that completely covered the crate. We then rejoined the convoy. Meyer made a map, carefully noting mileage, etc. I never saw Meyer or the map again, for he was

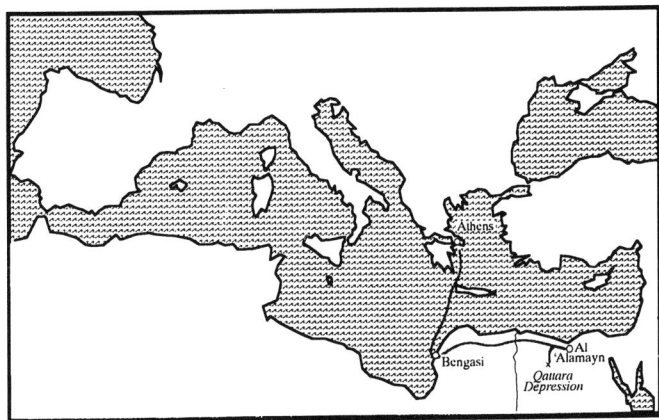

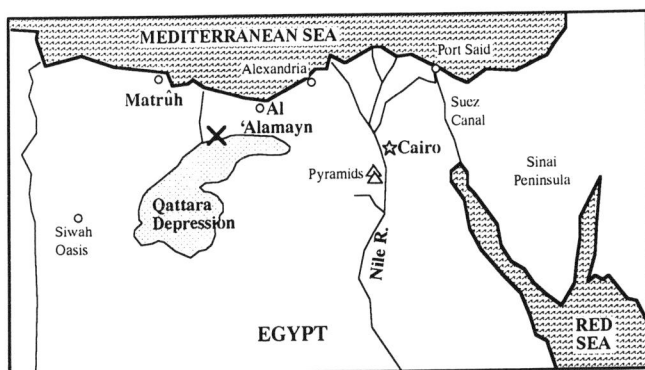

70

killed when our truck hit one of the mines set by our own men. I was hospitalized, but recovered nicely.

"Now I have emphysema and don't have many years left. I've been longing to visit my many friends buried at Al Alamayn but had about given up hope. I'm certain that the skeleton is still there and I don't need a map. I'll lead you to it if you'll take me on your expedition. A few men could recover it in a couple of days. . . . "

"I'll have to think about that. After all, we don't know if the specimen is still there and I don't even know if it's something that would be of interest to me. You couldn't be an official member of the expedition so your travel would have to be paid by a private source. I just don't know if I could put it all together. I'll think about it, however," I promised.

We exchanged phone numbers, and the next day I took my amazing story to the graduate dean. He was my good friend and mentor. He was also the driving force behind most of the research on campus.

When I finished, he queried, "What do you think?"

"I haven't the foggiest. It may be more something that would interest Fred." Fred is an archaeologist at the university who excavates a lot in the Middle East. "I'll tell you what, I can handle his expenses after we arrive in Egypt, and I can get his round trip passage for about $1,000. If I had it to spare on my own I'd take a chance. Its a long shot, but might be a great discovery."

"That's good enough for me. I'll find the money for his airline ticket. Keep me posted. If you get something good, it will go better for my rerouting the $1,000."

Voss was ecstatic when I told him it was "Go." Wayne and I had to find another place to meet on

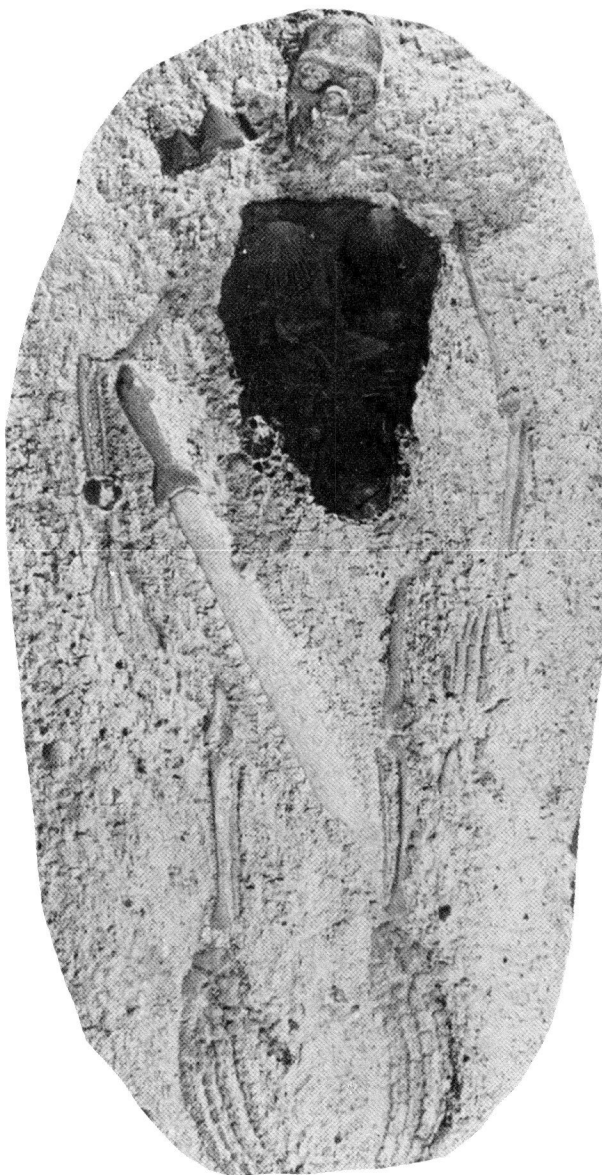

Figure 38 *Remains of Neptunoides*

Figure 39 *Neptunoides' sword.*

Tuesday evenings when we wanted to talk, for Wilhelmwas always at the Rose waiting to rehash our plans.

Finally the day came. I'll say one thing for Wilhelm: he certainly knows how to pack light. When we picked him up at his home, he had a single suitcase plus a small carry-on. We were met at the Cairo airport by my good friend Dr. Bahay Issawi, probably the best geologist in Egypt. When I introduced Wilhelm and gave a brief sketch of the story, Bahay sort of rolled his eyes as if to say, "Sucker!"

Wilhelm caught this gesture and immediatley began to make his case to Bahay. I interrupted with, "There'll be plenty of time for stories when we get on the way."

Happily, Bahay had already arranged for desert permits, and and the crew assembled and the trucks packed. There were only a couple of stops to pick up some perishables and we were on our way the next day. There were two Russian jeeps and one large stake bed truck carrying the equipment. Wilhelm, Bahay, the driver and myself were in one jeep. As soon as we were on the road I told Bahay that I'd like to stop in Alexandria overnight. That would give me time to photograph a really nice Cretacious fish collection on deposit at the museum there. I had been telling a paleoichthyologist about them for a couple years. Bahay was willing but Wilhelm protested that he wanted to press on to Al Alamayn.

"I'm sorry Wilhelm, but the first order of business is the science we are being paid for," I explained.

Bahay spoke up, "Since you want to spend time in Al Alamayn, the truck and other jeep can press on, and we'll meet you tomorrow afternoon at the German Cemetery."

I always admired Bahay's ability to work out

messy details. That pleased Wilhelm no end. It would give him a full day in Al Alamayn.

When we arrived at the German Cemetery, I went inside alone and was very touched to find Wilhelm kneeling almost in the middle of the massive field of headstones. I had visited the British Cemetery several times but must admit this was my first visit here. By far the majority of headstones gave the age of the dead soldier as between 17 and 23, row upon row. One wonders how a nation recovers from such carnage. The emotions of the war years had vanished and the effect of this visit was no different on me than visits to the cemeteries of our allies in that war.

"Wilhelm, we have to press on. Each day here costs us a great deal of money," I said with my hand on his shoulder.

"I know." He looked up with tears streaming down his face. Pointing to a grave nearby, he said, "This was my best boyhood friend. We attended college together." I had been maintaining control until then but could hold it no longer. We embraced briefly and then emerged from the cemetery gate arm in arm. In our country this might have been mistaken as a strange gesture, but in Egypt male friends stroll arm in arm all the time.

We drove along the coast of the Mediterranean for a while and then up onto the flat that separates the coast from the Qattarah Depression. We continued west but at a slightly higher elevation until we came to a faint trackway lined with rocks on either side. When we started turning, Wilhelm was uncertain.

"It was a much better traveled road and there were no rock liners."

Bahay explained that the road was hardly ever used today and the rock liners are to keep vehicles from venturing off the road. Only the road had been swept clear of uncharted mines set by the Germans when they were retreating forty years earlier. The extremely dry climate had preserved the deadliness of many of the mines, which were often heard to go off early in the morning when the temperature was changing rapidly.

Bahay added, "Believe me, this is the only access to the depression between Al Alamayn and Matruh."

When one drives across this featureless flat and then is introduced to the depression suddenly, it's sort of like one's first view of the Grand Canyon. The vastness and bleakness of this huge basin of rocks and huge sand dunes is very nearly unbelievable. We stopped at the top of the escarpment and Wilhelm looked worried.

"The road was straight and descended at a steeper angle," he explained anxiously.

Bahay was sure that the road had been "improved" and as we descended, we could see the old road to our left. It had been eroded almost into a gully. The new path took the road to the west, fortunately, or it might have encountered our specimen. When we stopped, Wilhelm hit the ground running, and almost immediately, yelled. After some exclamation in German, he got back to English, "I told you it would still be here!"

Fortunately for us, most of the sand and rock had long since washed, or more likely, blown away. The crate sort of hung precariously in the narrow ravine some eight feet above the bed. With some shovel work we were able to back the truck almost under the crate. It was then a simple matter to slowly dig the sand and rock from under the corners, letting it down softly into the truck. We could clearly see "Field Marshal ROMMEL" and "AFRIKA KORPS" stenciled on top of the crate. Wilhelm wanted to open it immediately but Bahay wisely said that he'd prefer not to have the men see it until we could evaluate the specimen. It was hard

Figure 40 *Shark teeth on sword*
Galeocerdo (left)
Hemipristis (right).

to drive on with our prize under the sealed lid. After following the escarpment a few miles to the area I wanted to prospect this season, we left the men to set up camp while Wilhelm, Bahay, and I took the truck and drove back to Cairo with our prize. We drove into the building where we store the equipment from year to year and opened the crate. As advertised, the face portion of a skull could be seen protruding from the shell conglomerate. Much of the skeleton was still buried in the shall hash but it clearly was a nearly complete skeleton. The individual was indeed wearing a breast plate that was made of copper or a copper alloy such as bronze. It had a few barnacles attached giving evidence that it had been under the sea for sometime, although the high point upon which the Temple of Posedion sits surely has not been under water since the advent of breast plates.

Well, we needed to get back to the business at hand. Bahay quickly made arrangements for permits to ship the specimen and we had it on its way before we returned to our camp.

Our season didn't go well and while many bones were discovered nothing was exactly what we had hoped for. So, my mind never wandered far from the Posedion specimen.

A couple of months after I returned home I got a call that the large crate had been delivered to the Houston Museum for me. I hooked the carryall up to a four by eight foot trailer and retrieved my prize. Our creature looked so regal in his bed of shell hash that it was decided to prepare it only to the extent that the skeleton and artifacts could be studied.

Neptunoides aquaticus, new genus and species
(Fig. 38)

Diagnosis: Feet with additional joints (hyperphalangy) not unlike the flippers of a seal.

Etymology: *Neptunoides* (very like

74

Neptune) + *aquaticus* (water dwelling).

Type locality: Temple of Posideon, Sounion, Greece (Fig. 37).

Age: I am tempted to assign our sea king to the domain of the Tethyan Sea since it once covered the area and is no more. However, a proper time to consider the Tethyan Sea extinct was the drying up of the Mediterranean Sea which was originally a part of Tethys. This would place the demise of our King around 5,000,000 years ago, before there were any men approaching the level of development of this individual. Furthermore, the advent of metal working, even wrought, was not much earlier than 10,000 B.P. (before present). Then there's the matter of the shell hash being so high above sea level. True, tectonic activity could have raised the point after fossilization, but I revisited the site and could find no other evidence of fossil shell hash in the area. I suspect that these remains were found, recognized, or perceived as a Sea King, brought to this point and either buried beneath the Temple of Posideon or the Temple was constructed over him as a tomb. Considering the options, this doesn't help in assigning a date for his death. It seems too fortuitous that the Temple was accidentally constructed over the burial site. This must be considered a Greek deity.

Description: The skeleton is decidedly different from that of a normal modern human. The skull is rather primitive in that the brow ridges are quite pronounced. The arms are normal but the legs have a strange proportion. The tibia-fibula (lower leg) is rather short relative to the length of the femur (thigh bone). This must be related to swimming although I would rather expect the opposite for swimming strength. It could be to partially offset the clumsiness of land locomotion on such flipper-feet. In any case, we have no analog with which to compare.

The flippers themselves are quite bizarre. Although they have the normal number of toes, the number of joints has increased from four to eight. Such a change through the usual evolutionary rates would take millions of years. If, on the other hand, *Neptunoides* is a result of crossing between creatures unknown to us, it could be a hybrid characteristic.

Artifacts: The breast plate is of copper or copper alloy (Fig. 41), considering the green patina. The metal is so thin as to afford little protection. I suspect it was native copper tooled over a wooden form and the wood has since rotted. It depicts an octopus embossed over the stomach area. A pair of fish flanking the head of the octopus and a pair of pecten shells above the breasts are either tooled or cast separately and added to the plate.

Of special interest is the sword (Fig. 39). The handle represents a scaly fish and is carved from a translucent material like travertine. The blade is carved from ivory and presents four more fish which are identical save diminishing size from point to haft. The edge of the blade is "sharpened" with shark teeth that are of great interest. The teeth near the haft and the point belong to the tiger shark (*Galeocerdo*, Fig. 40) which still lives in the area. The teeth arming the main portion of the blade however, belong to the genus (*Hemipristis*, Fig. 40). *Hemipristis* occur around the Mediterranean as fossils but is restricted to the Indian Ocean today. This leaves two options (1) that the teeth were collected as fossils and placed in the sword millions of years after the death of the sharks or (2) somehow *Neptunoides* made it around the tip of Africa and collected the teeth in the Indian Ocean. The teeth don't look fossilized but this would certainly be the easiest explanation.

Lying partially buried in the shell hash to the right of his head is a crown of sorts. It is a copper

75

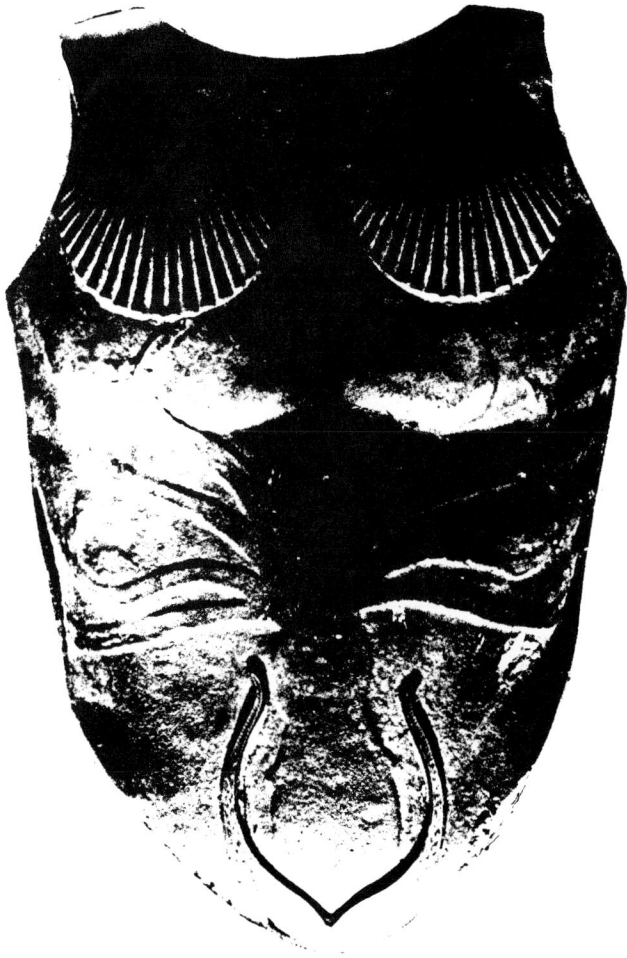

band embossed with stylized waves and decorated with three teeth of the shark *Carcharadon megalodon*, the largest shark ever known. Teeth of this species occur in Miocene and Pliocene age deposits worldwide. These were certainly fossils when added to the crown as the species has been extinct for some 7,000,000 years.

On his right wrist is a bronze bracelet of intertwined crabs, the symbol of Posideon— another bit of evidence that we are indeed dealing with the Greek deity. However, all writings and images of the Greek Deity have him carrying a trident instead of a sword. I feel that *Posideon*, or *Neptune* to the Romans, may not be the only Sea King. If this creature was King only of the Tethys Sea, it may or may not be related to *Posideon*. The Greeks must have thought differently, however, since he was either buried beneath the Temple or the Temple was built over him.

Conclusions: *Neptunoides* was an aquatic-adapted hominoid, who apparently died and was laid, or came to rest, in a bed of shell hash along with his armor and weapon. The burial site was either below sea level or later sank below sea level as evidenced by the growth of barnacles on the breast plate. Sometime later his remains were discovered by the ancient Greeks and recognized, or perceived, as a Sea King and removed to higher ground at Sounion and the Temple of Posedion.

Figure 41 *Neptunoides' breast plate.*

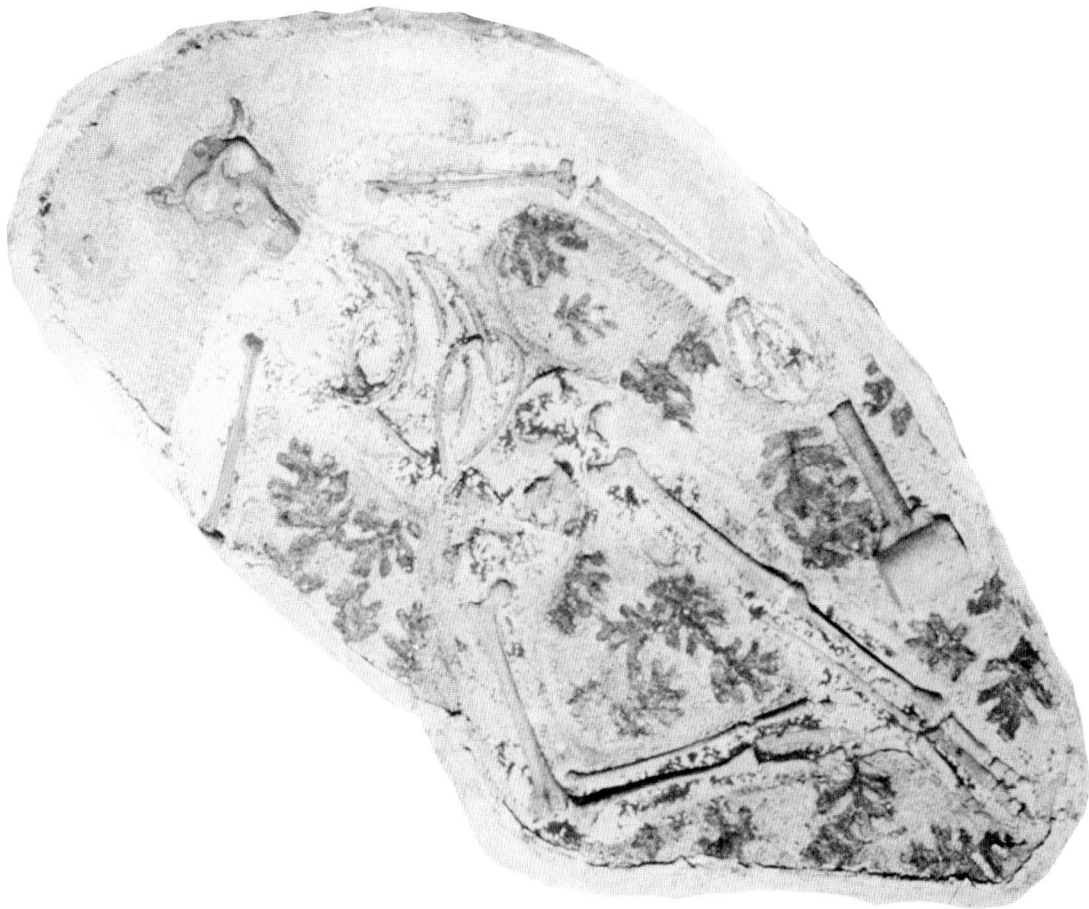

Figure 42 *Oni skeleton.*

ONI

My graduate students and I were at a little pub near the campus discussing a theory concerning Asia being the area of origin of Caucasians, with the arrival of the Mongoloid race not until about 18,000 years ago. One of the prime points of the hypothesis is that the Ainu people of northern Japan are clearly Caucasian and were the first people in Japan. I had told the group the week before that this would be our topic, and an artist friend who often attends our sessions had brought a Japanese-American artist with him. During the discussion this young man, Yoichi Aoki, told us about his fascination with the Ainu when he lived in Japan. He had even made the trip to Hokkaido Island in northern Japan where most of the few pure blood Ainu live today, just to see them. I had never known anyone who had seen the Ainu, and arranged to meet Yoichi later for a private discussion.

The next day, I met Yoichi at the same pub for lunch, and my questions began. He was very observant, a trait of a good artist, which made his descriptions most interesting. I had been invited to make a lecture tour in Japan a few months hence, so I asked Yoichi to tell me how to get to Hokkaido and other logistical data that would make my quest easier.

"When will you be there?" he asked.

"My three lectures will be in May, but I hope to pack them all into one week so I can have a week to visit Hokkaido."

"I have a gallery opening there June 15th and perhaps I could change my agenda and go a little early, and we could visit the Ainu together," Yoichi said. Such luck I had never hoped for. Not only does Yoichi know the area and the people, but the language, and seemed a very interesting and fun fellow to travel with. I could hardly wait.

The morning of my last lecture there was a message at my hotel:

> CAN'T LEAVE UNTIL DAY AFTER
> TOMORROW. CHECK OUT AND I
> WILL PICK YOU UP AROUND
> TEN A.M. SATURDAY MORNING
> IN FRONT OF YOUR HOTEL.
> YOICHI

The trip was an adventure in itself. We rode the train to the most northern point of the main island and then caught a ferry over to Muroran on the island of Hokkaido. There we rented a small car and made our way north to the city of Sapporo. We then drove straight to the most concentrated population of the Ainu. It was clear that considerable Oriental genes had become incorporated into the Ainu population over the past few thousand years, but there were a few individuals who would go unnoticed on any middle European street, if clean-shaven and dressed in western style. My story is getting far afield, I fear, but this was the way we met old Tatsuo.

Yoichi was showing me the open air market in Sapporo when we stopped to look at some local folk art. There was a sprinkling of antiques in the collection, and Yoichi asked if the vendor ever got

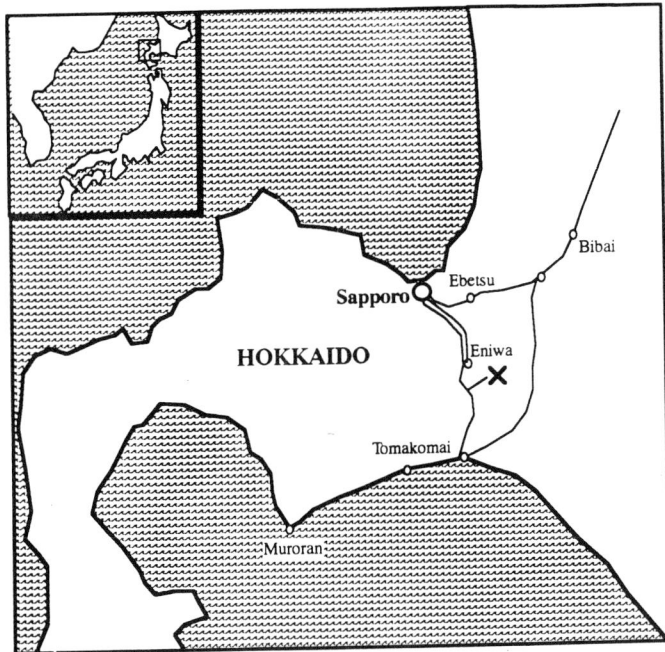

Figure 43 *Oni locality.*

any antique sculpture. He said no, but then added that perhaps we should see an old farmer in the market named Tatsuo. Then he unfolded a strange story.

"A month or so back Tatsuo showed me an arm of a statue for evaluation. The strangest thing was one could see bones protruding from the broken end. I've never heard of statues with skeletons inside."

We found old Tatsuo at the market. He had a booth set up selling fresh corn. Yoichi asked him about the arm of the statue.

"You interested in buying it?" Tatsuo asked.

"Perhaps. Where can we see it?" Yoichi replied after translating the question to me.

The old man drew a little map and told us to come Sunday. That was two days hence so we decided to press on northward and return Sunday. Tatsuo's home was a picture book of what one might think a rural Japanese farm house would look like. The house was made of thick, squared timbers. The roof was tile and double pitched, like so many I've seen in Canada. This is to disallow a thick accumulation of snow. He invited us in and poured some tea. He then left the room, and returned with the object wrapped in a towel. When he laid it out on the table and carefully unwrapped it, I was amazed. It did indeed look like the forearm and hand made of soft stone (Fig.45). Only one side was preserved as if it were split from elbow to the tips of the fingers, presenting only the upper surface. The ulna and radius (forearm bones) were protruding from the elbow area and one broken finger displayed finger bones inside as well. I was pretty sure I knew what it was. I have seen specimens at Pompeii where people had been buried by volcanic ash which made molds of the living form when the bodies decayed. Anthropologists have developed techniques whereby they pump plaster into these hollows and produce casts of the ancient people as they appeared in the flesh. Apparently this individual had been encased in ash, decayed, and then the mold was later partially filled with a fine grained sediment mixed with ash. I was excited, because fossils of the Ainu are essentially unknown, and if this was one, the ash could be potassiumn-argon dated and it would be most important to our knowledge of the peopling of the Japanese Islands.

I asked Yoichi to inquire as to the circumstances of the discovery and if he would show us the site. Tatsuo became very animated when Yoichi asked, and began pulling on his rubber boots. Yoichi told me that the old man said we would get our feet wet. This didn't matter at that point. We were wearing canvas shoes. We walked down a narrow road until we got to a calendar-picture arched stone bridge. We climbed down the bank and began wading upstream. The stream was narrow, but had steep banks and was so deep we could not see out of the cut while walking. Soon enough we encountered a pool formed by water coming over a waterfall about eight feet tall. Tatsuo pointed to the pool and Yoichi translated that the arm was found in the fall side of the pool. It was clear that it must have eroded out of the escarpment. The vertical face was covered with moss and fern, but here and there some of the moss had dropped off exposing a deposit of nearly white ash. It was capped by a sort of freshwater marl that was much more resistant and this was what formed the fall itself. Once the marl is breached, the ash would erode away quickly. Yoichi asked Tatsuo if the falls had receded much in his lifetime.

"Yes, about ten meters," he said sadly.

I knew we would have to break through the capping marl to excavate the specimen and that would cause an immediate upstream migration of the falls of about ten feet. Yoichi relayed this and the old man frowned. This turned into a smile, however, when we told him we would probably be able to pay damages of about one hundred dollars.

The first step was to trowel off the moss so we could see if there was indeed any more of the specimen there. We encountered the distal end of the humerus (upper arm bone), so we decided to take a chance. It would be quite an excavation and would require picks, shovels, buckets, and lots of plaster. The breaching of the capping marl would require a sledgehammer. Then there was the problem of the water running over the excavation. Nevertheless, the following day we arranged for the tools and materials plus lots of plaster. We left it to Tatsuo to hire two helpers. We rerouted the stream

81

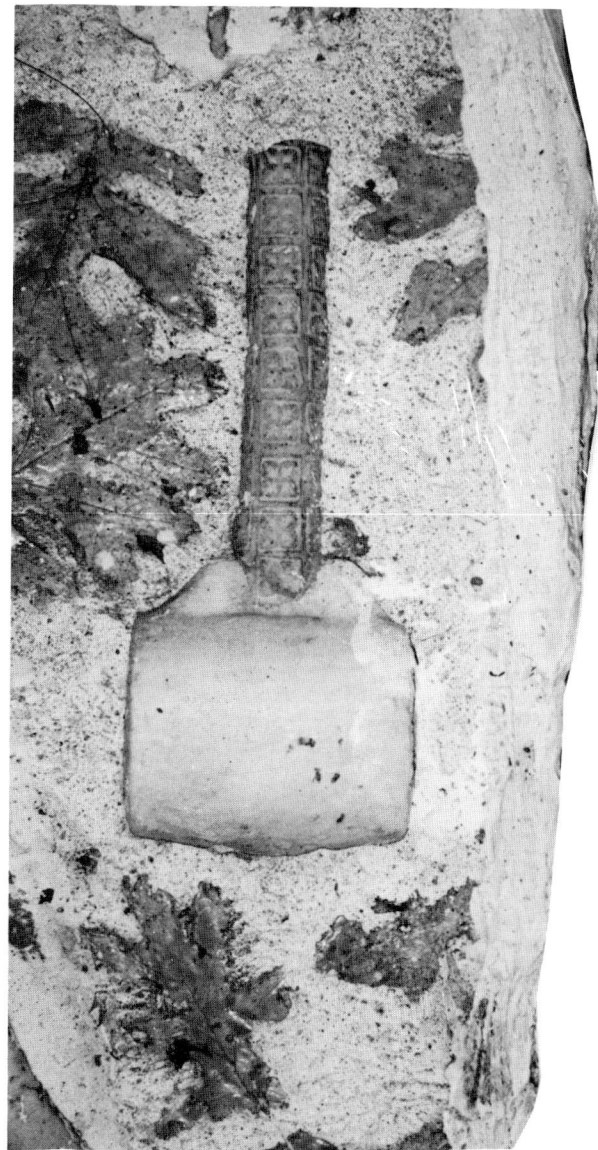

Figure 44 *Oni's mallet.*

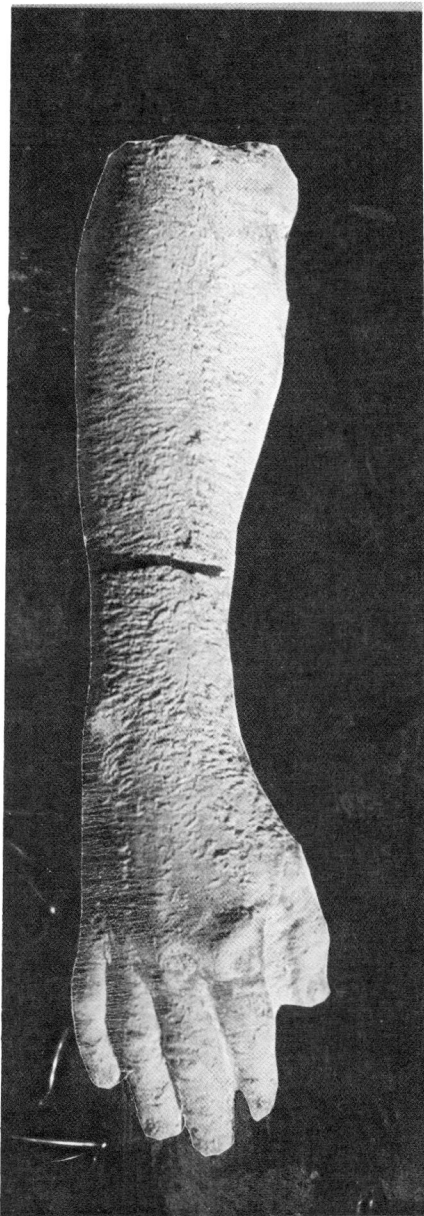

Figure 45 *Oni's arm.*

as far as we could to one side, packing dirt up into a dike separating the new stream route and our excavation. We then broke through the marl and began to excavate carefully. I could tell that much humor accompanied the digging, but the conversation moved slowly for me as Yoichi didn't translate things he considered unimportant, leaving me to wonder.

Fortunately, the ash deposit was relatively light colored and the filling of the mold was darker. We could therefore tell when we were approaching the skeleton from one side. The bones were not completely encapsulated in the mold filling so apparently the mold never quite filled. Therefore, only the backside of the individual was cast. The up or front side was merely the skeleton as it settled in the mold. The ash is somewhat lighter than most rock so the entire block weighted less than five hundred pounds after it was plastered. When we returned to Tokyo we opened the block and pared it down to perhaps four hundred pounds, replastered and shipped it home. We had to get antiquity permits and promised to return it to Japan if it turned out to be something new to science. This would have taken several weeks had I not remembered Teruya Uyeno, a Japanese vertebrate paleontologist I had met when he was a graduate student at the University of Michigan. He is now at the National Museum in Tokyo and managed to rush things along.

"New to science" was an understatement. When the specimen was prepared, a very bizarre creature emerged. The skull was hominoid but rather primitive, about the level of *Homo erectus*. In addition, the creature had rather large horns on the anterior portions of parietal bones. Equally as astounding are the feet— they have but three toes. It doesn't look as though they are deformed. Each toe has a small hoof, not unlike those of tapir or rhinoceros. Associated with the fossil is a single artifact, a mallet. The head is of ivory and the decorated handle is carved of bone (Fig. 44).

After considerable discussion in Japanese, Yoichi and Ted turned to me and announced that our specimen had all the prerequisites of being an *Oni*. Although *Oni* are still believed in by some but rural folk, most "enlightened" people would laugh at the suggestion. *Oni* are demons or devils that caused people a lot of problems in bygone days. They are said to be ugly and not very smart, but mean as hell. They raped the women and hit the men on the head with their mallets. And last but not least, they have but three toes. I had to admit this certainly sounded like our creature.

Oni aoki, new genus and species
Figure 43

Type specimen: LU 60324; Complete skeleton plus cast of the rear half of the body as it appeared in the flesh.

Diagnosis: Skull primitive with approximately 1100 cubic centimeters of volume; Fairly large horns placed on the pariatal bones; three toed foot, not unlike that of a tapir; stood about 5'1" tall and arms long relative to the legs.

Type locality: Beneath the waterfall on the Tatsuo Farm 30 miles south of the city of Sapporo, Japanese Island of Hokkaido (Fig. 42).

Etymology: *Oni* (The ancient vernacular name) + *aoki*, in honor of Youchi Aoki, friend and scholar.

Discussion: Long before the stream developed, this must have been a shallow pond. The *Oni* was buried by volcanic ash approximately 4,000 years ago. The event probably occurred in the fall as the varve corresponding to the burial time has many impressions of leaves of deciduous oak trees. The leaves appear to have been stripped green from the trees. Air turbulence of the volcanic eruption that rained the ash might be responsible. The *Oni's* body deteriorated and the mold was partially filled by a sandy sediment washing in, perhaps through a crack. The valley continued to fill with sediments until downcutting by the stream encountered the remains.   The mallet (Fig. 44) is well made with the head carved of elephant or perhaps mammoth ivory. It has buttresses fore and aft strengthening its placement on the bone handle. The handle is beautifully carved with a redundant design.

The cast of the upper portion of the right arm shows that the individual was fairly old and wrinkled (Fig. 45). The horns are bovine-like and larger than those of *Pan* and unlike the sheep-like horns of the American *Pan*-like character, *Kokopelli*. I know of no fringe homonoid, however, with perissodactyl-like foot. All other ungulate-hominoids have the artiodactyl-like hooves. *Oni* are said to have shown up in Japan with the introduction of Buddhism but the dates suggest they were there long before. Encounters with *Oni* have fallen off considerably since World War II, making most Japanese very skeptical of their existence.

PACIFIC MERMAID

y friend, Dr. Shelton Applegate, is a paleoichthyologist at the Instituto de Paleontologia in Mexico City. As a colleague, he has done considerabl work in Latin America on both fossil and recent sharks. I wrote to him when I was planning an expedition to Panama. Although I would be seeking fossils of Miocene rodents in terrestrial deposits, the Gatune Formation just below, had produced a number of fossil fish. I asked if there were any localities he would like me to check. Shelly wrote back that I should watch my stratigraphy closely. It seems that exposures in the canal banks show lots of channel filling of various ages, some quite young. Apparently it is near enough to the sea that each lowering of sea level allowed rivers to cut deep canyons and when the sea came back they filled with sediment at different times. I filed that information and off we went.

Our geologist friends in Panama, Bob and Jay Stewart, took us straight to a wonderful road cut that exposed the sediments of the desired age and we immediately found bone scrap and freshwater fish teeth. We began to excavate the clay, dry it in the sun, and then wet sieve it in the canal. One day graduate student Jennifer Lezak took a break and waded down the canal looking at exposures of what we presumed to be the Miocene Gatune Formation. After a while, we heard her calling and saw her a couple hundred yards away waving her arms.

Another graduate student, Phil Murry, and I hurried along the shallows to Jennifer. She had already washed a slab of mudstone and looked quizzical as she sputtered and pointed. There was a school of what could be nothing else but tiny mermaids on the slab (Fig.l)! We counted thirty-four complete and partial individuals and the way the slab was broken, there may originally have been hundreds. This slab was loose in the shallows, but didn't look as though it had washed far. Even so, our search did not reveal the source of the slab. However, wading some distance downstream, we discovered a number of smaller slabs containing remains of the same species in the shallows. Several different colored sediments and bone preservation types probably represent different times and conditions. Apparently, this area was a place where numerous die offs, or catastrophes, have happened. I then realized that whatever mermaids were, they were certainly too humanoid to be Miocene in age. So, remembering Shelly's warning, Phil, Jennifer, and I

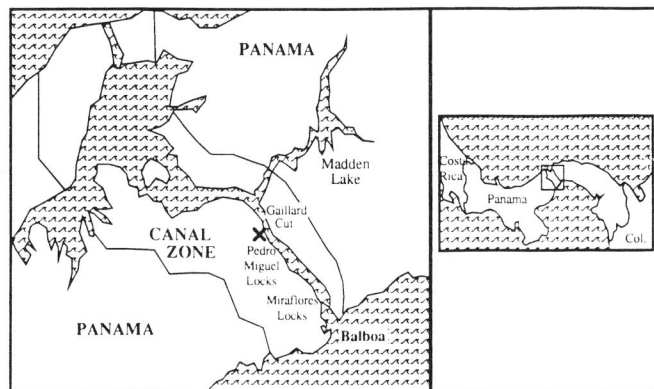

Figure 46 *Pacific Mermaid locality.*

Figure 47 *Crew washing slabs containing fossil remains.*

began to clean the vegetation off the immediate bank so we could see the stratigraphy. Sure enough, we found the edge of a channel fill with Miocene oysters on one side and modern snails on the other. We collected enough of the shell from each side to run radiocarbon dates. We packed our specimens and returned home with the bonus.

The deposits we knew to be Gatune dated beyond the range of radiocarbon dating and the dates on materials from the channel fill from which we think the mermaids came range from 2050 to 2177 years before the present. By the way, we got the wanted Miocene rodents, as well.

Back at my labs at Ladonia University, I cleaned the specimens better. I found several striking differences between these mermaids and the one known from Texas. The Panamanian mermaids have much longer tails. It's not unlike comparing the skeletal remains of a long fish, such as a pike, with those of a short fish, like a perch. The tail of the Texas specimen has a primitive but developing hyplural fan (bony tailfin support, Fig. 51A), while the hyplurals in the Panama form are much less well developed (Fig. 51B). These two aquatic hominoids are clearly different enough to be designated as different genera.

Homicthoides applegati, new genus and species
Figs. 48, 49

Holotype: LU 61553. Slab containing 34 complete and partial skeletons.

Type Locality: Channel fill in exposure of the Gatune Formation in the North Bank of the Panama Canal west of the Pedro Miguel locks (Fig. 46).

Diagnosis: Smaller and longer than *Homicthys*, probably much more flexible; tail support primitive but upper body equal in hominoid development in both genera. The teeth are very different from human teeth and those of the Atlantic

86

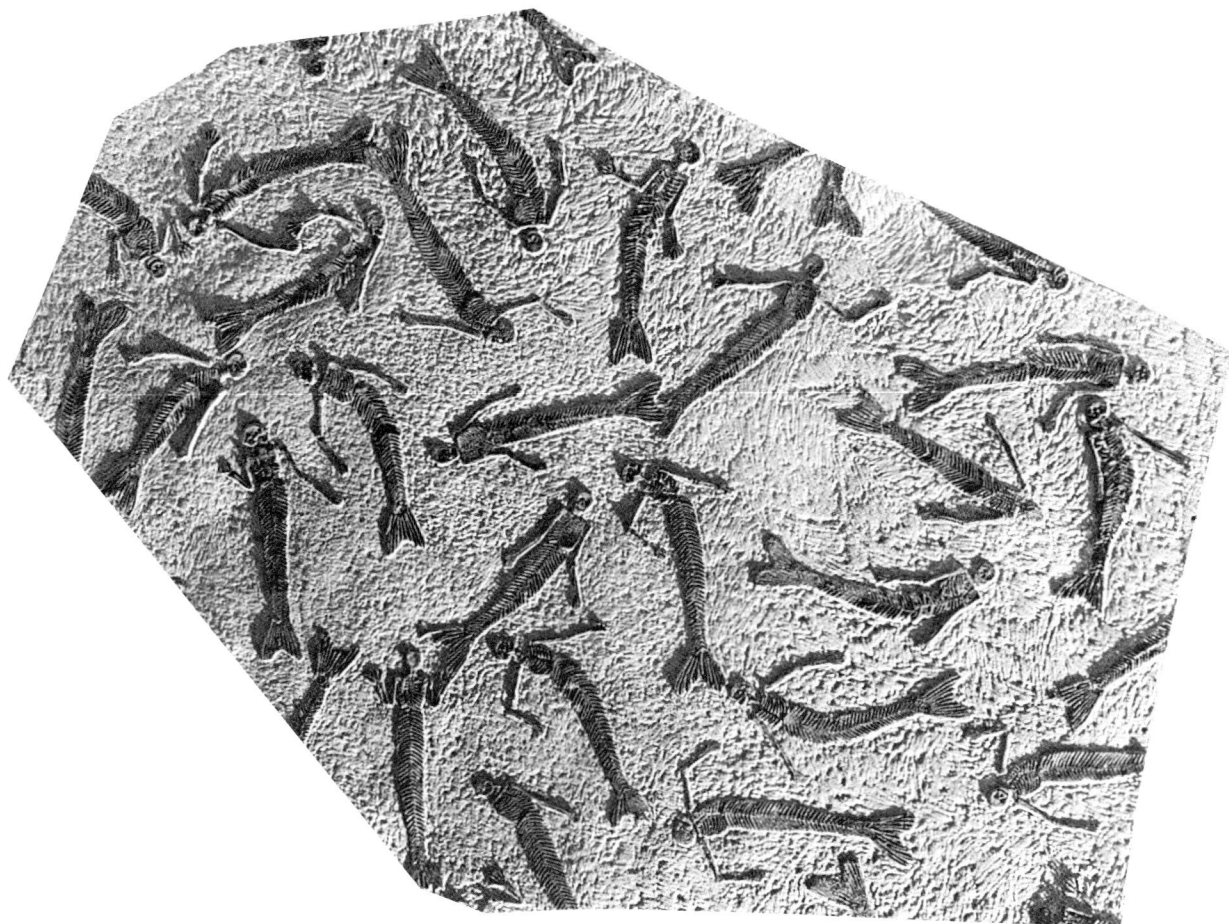

Figure 48 *Pacific Mermaid skeletons.*

Figure 49 *Close-up of Pacific Mermaid.*

Mermaid. They are leaf-shaped and serrate, very like those of marine iguanas (Fig. 50). These are obviously specialized for the eating of seaweed and perhaps soft bodied invertebrates, such as hermit crabs and worms. Those of the Atlantic mermaid are very human-like (bunodont) ideal for a very varied diet. Several of the individuals show webbing between the fingers as, of course, one might expect in such swimming creatures.

Etymology: *Homicthys* + *oides* (like) = Mermaid like *Homicthys* but not exactly + *applegati* named for my scholarly friend Dr. Shelton Applegate.

Age: Two radiocarbon dates were run on material from the channel fill believed to have produced our specimens. One sample, a clam, produced a date of 2050 years Before Present +/- 175 years. Shell dates tend to be a little young. The other test, vegetative stems, produced a date of 2177 +/- 250. The dates overlap, giving us confidence in their accuracy. It's interesting to note that channel filling on the Texas Coastal Plain often produces dates in this range.

Discussion: Although the two known examples of mermaids known (Gulf of Mexico and tropical Pacific) do not prove the point, it is more common for perch-shaped fishes to be more isolate in their behavior and the Gulf Mermaids both have been found in singles. Elongated marine fishes, on the other hand, tend to be more of the schooling type as is the case with these Pacific Mermaids.

Another interesting fact is that this assemblage seems to be all female. Statistically, this would beimpossible in any normal population. There seem to be two possibilities: (1) That their reproduction stratigy is like that certain Blenny fishes. In these fish populations there is but a single male and when he dies, one of the remaining females turns into a male. Or, (2) schooling divides populations by size and sex, as in some sharks Galeorhinus.

The new form adds nothing to our knowledge of the origin of these amazing creatures that seem part fish and part human. However, the fact that there are at least two genera indicates that they had a long evolution. Of course, if these creatures come and go between dimensions and are only occasionally caught in ours at the moment of death, we may never have a complete enough fossil record to lead us to their origins.

The station wagon we rented for our work in Panama was so small there was no room for our shovels inside. We therefore duct-taped them to the rear bumper. Each time we would stop for gasoline or to ask directions, people would make playful comments about us being grave robbers. No matter how much I protested this label and tried to explain our venture, they could not be convinced that we were not after huacas. Although against the law, lots of people search out the ancient graves and dig them up for the huacas, small gold figures of men, gods or small animals such as frogs. One evening I was socializing at the Balboa Yacht Club when I met an interesting archeologist, Dr. Roberto DeLarios. When I discovered his speciality was huacas, I told him about our being branded grave robbers.

A

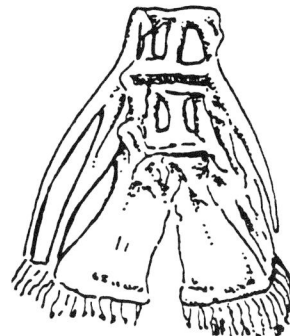

B

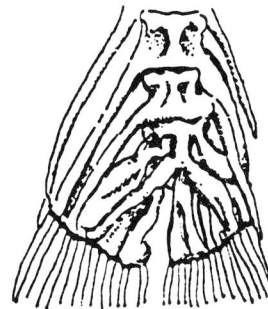

Figure 50 *Teeth of Pacific Mermaid.*

Figure 51 *(A) Tail of Atlantic Mermaid*
(B) Tail of Pacific Mermaid.

89

"You do excavate human remains, do you not?" he asked.

"Not normally. However, this trip we were lucky enough to uncover a group, or perhaps I should say school, of fossil mermaids."

Roberto became very interested and said that this may answer several questions that had plagued him. He began, "A few years ago I collected a silver necklace. It features skeletons of mermaids. As I recovered it while excavating, I'm certain that it has some antiquity but its probably not Mayan as it is made of silver. All of the burial offerings I've seen are of gold. This made me wonder if the piece might not have been imported from some other area. And why would the silversmith depict skeletons rather than mermaids in the flesh? I also wondered if the piece might not be Spanish. After all, mermaids are from Mediterranean Mythology are they not? Now, however, I realize that the silversmith simply saw some fossils such as you have discovered and it fired his imagination. Therefore I suppose the specimen could be the work of either ancients or Spaniards."

The actual specimen was locked away in a vault somewhere but Roberto had negatives and said he would have some photos made for me. The following day some wonderful 8x10s were delivered to our quarters and there could be no doubt the silver replicas (Fig. 52) represent the same species as our fossils. They even depicted the same number of vertebrae. The outcrop that produced all the Panamanian fossil mermaids was exposed by the excavation of the Panama Canal but it would now appear that there are other natural outcrops in the area that produce fossil mermaids.

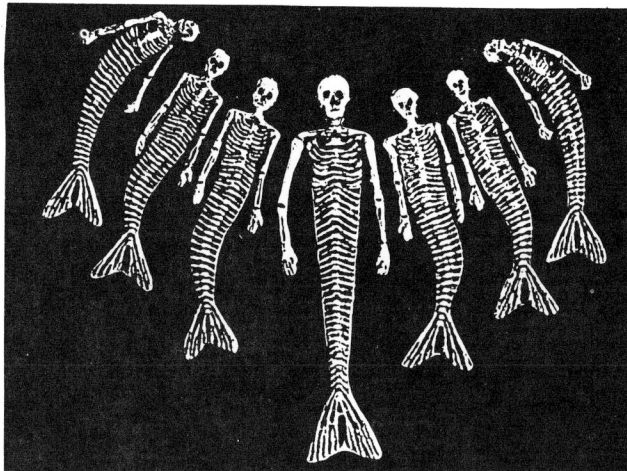

Figure 52 *Silver replicas of Pacific Mermaids.*

DEAD PAN

ach fall I used to spend several days at the Smithsonian Institution looking at teeth of whatever mammals held my interest at the time. In 1968, I was looking at squirrel teeth. The summer before I had collected a number of fossil squirrel teeth from Miocene age deposits along the Texas Gulf Coast. I was in my assigned work space surrounded by stacks of trays containing the skulls of flying squirrels, tree squirrels, and ground squirrels from all over the world. In the distance, but coming closer, I heard the voice of Dr. Clayton Ray, Curator, talking. Soon enough, there he was with a tall bearded man who was smiling and extending his hand in my direction.

"Professor Slaughter, I'm pleased to meet you. I've read a few of your papers and we have some thoughts in common."

Dr. Ray interrupted, "Bob Slaughter, Bill Waldren. Bill is an archeologist from Mallorca. He's here studying the ever-growing incisors (front teeth) of South American camels. I have a luncheon meeting and thought you two would have enough in common to share lunch somewhere."

"That's great. I hate to eat alone and I'm starving. What's your pleasure, Bill, cafeteria or fast food?" I said, putting my jacket on.

He winced when I said fast food, so I headed toward the Castle, a term of affection for the original Smithsonian Building which now serves as the lunch spot. As we walked toward the Castle, I queried him about his studies.

"What's someone from Mallorca doing studying South American camels?" I asked

"While doing archaeological excavations in caves and rock shelters on Mallorca, I recovered large numbers of bones of Myotragus, the small goat-like antelope. They are the only other artiodactyl (cloven hoofed) that has ever-growing incisors. I'm just making a comparison between them."

During lunch I told Bill more than he wanted to know about squirrels, so when he began to yawn, I switched to my other interest. "I'm also very interested in fossils that seem to represent creatures that are thought to be mythical."

"I'm glad you told me that," he said with a twinkle in his eye, "I just may have one for you."

"You have a unicorn?" I baited.

"Last year I had several groups of amateur archaeologists from the U.S. helping me with my excavations. At one end of the largest shelter is a

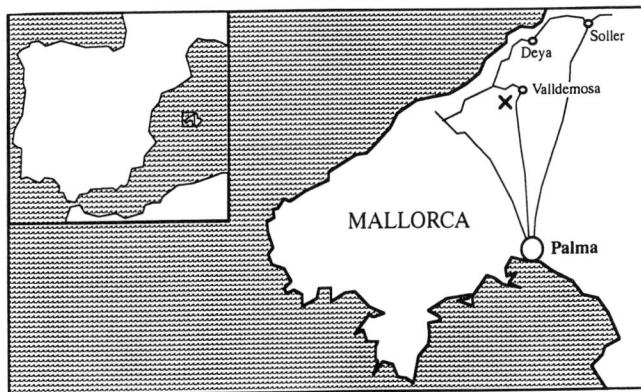

Figure 54 *Satyr locality.*

93

Figure 55 *Rock shelter producing remains of the satyr.*

huge boulder that fell from the ceiling millennia ago. When we had pretty well carved up the sedimentary profile except for that under the sedimentary profile except for that under the boulder, a medical doctor in the group kept tunneling under it. I told him several times that it was too dangerous and I didn't want him to continue. A couple days before the group was to leave I missed the good doctor and went to the boulder. Sure enough,there he was with only his feet sticking out of his burrow. I lost patience and pulled him from the hole by his heels. He interrupted my berating him to say excitedly that there was a human skull down there with horns. I took his flashlight and slithered down the hole. I returned saying that it was merely an outsized Myotragus with the nasals broken away. He was disappointed but didn't argue. Actually, it was human, or at least hominoid, but I just couldn't allow further excavation under this huge stone. I had him backfill the hole but I have been pondering the problem of how to move a hundred ton stone ever since. Any ideas?"

"How about explosives?" I suggested.

"I just don't know enough about them. Do you want to come over and make the recovery?" he offered.

"For the skull of the devil? Are you kidding? I'll be in Egypt in January and could come back by there then. Do you have access to an electric hammer drill and a power source?" I inquired.

"I can rent a generator but I don't know about a hammer drill."

"I can ship mine over before I leave for Egypt and it should be there by the time I arrive," I suggested.

When I arrived in Palma in early February, Bill was there to meet me. He apologized about the cold damp weather.

"Its par for this time of the year," he added.

Figure 56 *Skull of Pan.*

"Not to worry. We're working in a rock shelter, right?"

"True but we have to get the equipment up a very steep slope and mud will really hinder our efforts. It hasn't rained yet. Perhaps we should at least get the generator and your drill up before it does," he said, which really meant, "Are you up to a climb right now?"

"Let's go," I said.

He was right. It was a real project and I doubt that we could have done it in the rain. We made it, however, and were ready to get started the following morning. That night, I explained my plan. I had used his drawings which were very accurate. I planned to drill a line of holes across the boulder where we wanted it to break. The huge stone stuck out over the steep slope in front of the shelter and I was hoping that when it cracked, that portion would drop and slide far enough to give us room.

"Did you get the dynamite?" I asked.

"Sure did, but the landowner asked that I not spread it around that we exploded it. It seems that several years ago he dynamited some stumps and a neighbor claimed the noise made some of his goats abort and wanted compensation. He prefers that there be but a single blast and that it's origin remain a mystery."

"Perhaps I'd better put in a few more holes then, if we're not to have a second chance."

It took two days just to drill the holes, but when we loaded the dynamite and wired it, I felt pretty good about it. We let her go early in the morning and it seemed like the echo lasted forever. As soon as the gravel stopped falling and the dust cleared a bit, we came out from behind our respective trees. It was perfect. The boulder cracked and the leading third slid down the slope about ten meters, taking out a fair-sized tree along the way. Bill held both thumbs up.

95

Figure 57 *Pan flute*.

Before we began the excavation, we took the generator and hammerdrill back to Bill's. That way, we couldn't be accused of being the dynamiters.

Back at the shelter I said, "Show me how a shelter is excavated. I sieve about fifty tons of clay each summer looking for the likes of squirrel teeth, but I'm sure you move much slower than that."

He just grinned.

The sediments were soft and he was at the skull in short order. I don't know what I expected but I really didn't think it would be as advertised, a horned human skull. Still, there it was! The skull looked rather Neanderthalish and was bright green. Bill explained that when bones get very hot from the slack lime used to cremate the burials, the surviving bones often turn green. He picked up some bone scrap to make his point.

The skull, and other bones, were embedded in a dark gray sandstone so when we ascertained the extent of the skeleton we simply chiseled through the one foot thick lens around the fossil. When we finished, we had a block that weighed nearly a half ton. It's a good thing the slope was downhill or we could not have done it. Bill scrounged up seven friends and we just slid it down and then muscled it onto the trailer. We just left it on the trailer during preparation. Bill had good tools and I stayed until I was satisfied that it was all uncovered. The right leg came through the underside of the lens and was missing for the most part. The rest was essentially complete.

After the specimen arrived in Texas and preparation began, we made the startling discovery that the bones are made of bronze. The green color was simply the patina. At first I thought the skeleton must have been made by some ancient sculptor. But why, and how did he get it into the rock? I recovered a piece of of the right femur from the

96

it wasn't some unusual replacement of the bone. This still seems the best solution, although I know of no mechanism for it. I've seen bones replaced by a sort of "fool's gold" but iron is a common element of ground water. This burning question remains, but it seems apparent that (1) It is not an artifact, and (2) either the bone has been replaced by some unknown mechanism or the creature produced and lived with bronze bones. Considerable weight would be added, so the latter seems extremely unlikely.

Homotragulus waldreni, new genus and species
Figs. 53, 56

Type specimen: LM 3457 Complete skeleton still in rock.

Diagnosis: Hominoid with small horns attached to the frontal skull element (Fig. 56). Normal upper body skeleton, but legs modified for artiodactyl-type feet (Fig. 58).

Type locality: Valdemosa rock shelter near Valdemosa, Mallorca (Fig. 54).

Etymology: *Homo* (man) + *tragulus* (horned artiodactyl, *i.e.* antelope) + waldreni after Dr. William Waldren, Director of the Deya Archaeological Museum, Deya, Mallorca.

Discussion: In the rock near the right hand is a ten-tube flute (Fig. 57), sometimes referred to as a Pan Flute. It is shaped like a reed flute but is made of silver. The remains of this creature closely match the descriptions of satyrs, horned goat-footed men of Greek and Roman mythology. They are said to live largely in forests and are very light of heart. By far the best known is *Pan*, who is said to be expert with the ten tube flute. I am tempted to suggest that our specimen is indeed *Pan*, in that there is a ten tube flute associated with the remains in the rock. I suppose it is possible that other satyrs played similar flutes, so this point seems insolvable. Nevertheless, until others are found, this

Figure 58 *Pan foot* .

97

is the most parsimonious view.

Age: As to the age of the fossil, wood embedded in the same lens produced a date between A.D. 300 and 500. Like so many of the other fringe homonoids, its demise seems to coincide with the dissolution of the culture that believed in them, in this case the Romans who inherited the belief from the Greeks.

RUGARU

I gave a lecture on extinction at Tulane University in New Orleans in the middle '70s, and as was my habit, I accompanied some graduate students to a pub near campus that afternoon for further discussions of fossils. When I got around to telling about the amazing fossils of the fringe hominoids, one young man's eyes lit up. He said that he knew where such a creature was to be found but figured no one would believe him so he had never mentioned it. His colleagues all laughed and he was genuinely embarrassed. I urged him to continue his story and reminded everyone that they should "never say never."

He identified himself as T-Jean Ledet and started the story as it was told to him by his father, Jacque, a cajun trapper in La Fourch Parish.

"It was the habit of the swamp men (trappers and fishermen) to rendezvous at Bayou Grand Caillou occasionally. They had built a brush arbor where they would socialize in the evenings while trapping and fishing the area. When old man Arceneaux didn't return one evening, everyone was worried. One of the men had already expressed concern after he heard what he said was a noise made by a *Rugaru*. According to Cajun legend, the *Rugaru* are sort of the Bigfoot of the swamps but are much more aggressive.

"It would have been impossible for old man Arceneaux to simply be lost, as this was his area and he knew it better than anyone. So when he had not returned by morning, the men formed a search party. Old man Arceneaux was never found but some of the men found tracks in the mud that they were convinced were those of a *Rugaru* because of their huge size. These creatures are said to stand some eight feet tall. The men armed themselves and put a pack of coon hounds on the trail. When the dogs were out of sight but making chase noises, the men settled back and listened. When the baying told the hounds were running by sight instead of smell, they jumped to their feet. A short time thereafter the baying stopped. About an hour later one of the hounds reappeared rather badly wounded, and the others never returned. The rest of the day was spent putting together a much larger pack with hounds to trail and wolf dogs to fight. They had done this before when a cougar had happened through the area.

"The next morning they returned to Bayou Grand Caillou and loosed the dogs. They were trailing immediately and within an hour they were running by sight once again. Three of the men were riding horseback this time and they took off in the direction of the baying. One of these men was not a local but a wealthy doctor from New Orleans. He had a very nice place nearby where he raised fine horses and hunting dogs.

"When these three men found the dogs they had something cornered in a quarter acre patch of dense brush. The older dogs seemed cautious but several of the doctor's half grown hounds he had brought along for the experience very noisily dashed straight in and after a few yelps fell silent. When his prize pups disappeared in this fashion, the

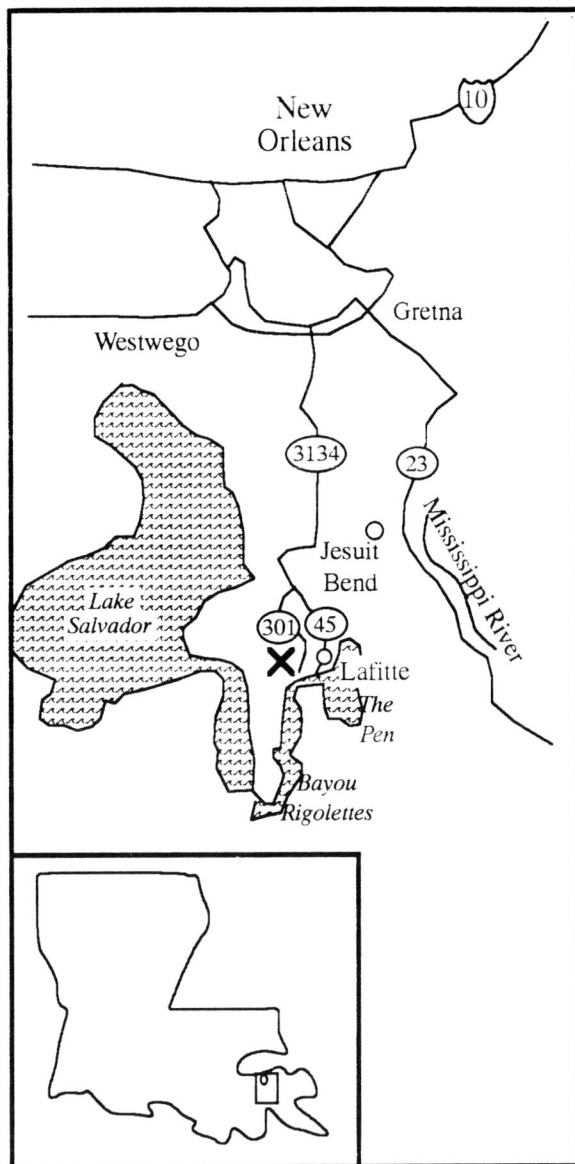

Figure 59 *Rugaru locality.*

doctor spurred his horse and rode right into the brush. He began firing his pistol and there was a great commotion. When the doctor staggered out sans horse, bleeding, and incoherent, the men opened fire with everything they had. Those on foot had arrived by then and the gunfire was withering. When things quieted down, the men cautiously probed the brush until they found their prey. Strewn about were the bodies of the pups and several adult dogs as well as the doctor's horse. After sitting in silence for a while starring at the beast, everyone agreed that it was a *Rugaru* even though no one had ever seen one before. It was rather human-like but huge and had large canine teeth protruding from its mouth. They had a discussion and decided not to make this incident known to thepublic, lest they get in trouble for killing the creature. After all, someone might take it for just an oversize human. Finally someone remembered an old well by an abandoned house on some high ground nearby and that's where they dumped the body. They estimated its weight at 500 pounds. Years later my dad took me to the well and shined a light down on the large skeleton in the dry well to prove what he had told me.

"'No guarantee that this was the only one around here so don't come back to this area,' my dad warned. 'There's plenty of other bayous to fish and hunt on.'"

T-Jean continued, "Years later when I came back from the service I took Old Man Arceneaux's grandson there to show him the bones but the well's brick walls had collapsed, burying the bones. Walking the levee back to the car we heard something splashing along in the bayou paralleling our path. Occasionally it would make the strangest noise. It reminded me a little of monkeys I'd heard in Viet Nam but much louder. We started running. The thing also moved faster and faster and we were

102

nearly panicked by the time we reached the car and sped away. I never returned."

I've investigated a number such stories around the world and only one of ten turns out to be as advertised, but one never knows.

"It's probably just a cow skeleton but let's check it out. How much debris do you think covers the skeleton?" I asked.

"I'm not sure, but now there's a road nearby and we could borrow my cousin's backhoe. It shouldn't take us more than an hour or two," T-Jean said.

The other students had stopped laughing and some wanted to go. T-Jean suggested that everyone with a gun arm themselves. I could tell his fear was genuine.

The old handmade bricks were so rotten the backhoe ate right through and easily removed full buckets of brick and clay as fast as we could get into the excavation to check for bone. When the well began to increase in diameter for the reservoir, T-Jean said that we must be close. The backhoe was abandoned and three of us went down in the hold and began removing brick and sediments by hand and buckets. Soon enough we encountered the bones of an outsized primate as the young man had said. I went straight for the skull and as I began to uncover it, I could see that it was no ordinary human. The large head has rectangular eye sockets and huge canine teeth. I've certainly never seen anything like it, human or otherwise. In a way the skull looked a little like a gorilla but the frontals are too inflated and the muzzle is not elongated as it is in the apes. Whether or not the stories told about the *Rugaru* are true, it's certainly not difficult to see where the stories came from.

We plastered the beast out and returned it to my lab at Ladonia University. I compared the bones with humans and other large apes and this specimen remains unique. I estimate it stood about seven and

Figure 60 *Rugaru skeleton.*

103

Figure 62 *Close-up of Rugaru skull.*

a half feet tall and had a massive chest. There's no way to tell how much of the body was covered with hair but *Rugaru* are said to be rather hairy. I was most impressed with the dentition. The teeth are of bear proportions and could do a great deal of damage in a fight.

Reported sightings of Rugaru have become almost a thing of the past. These creatures must have become more rare than they were long ago. This one was killed in 1921. Its description follows.

Rugaru ledeti, new genus and species
Figs. 60, 61

Type specimen: LU 67833. More or less complete skeleton of a male individual in its prime.

Etymology: *Rugaru*, named for the legend it gave rise to + *ledeti* for T-Jean Ledet, whose recollections of a childhood story led us to the beast. *Rugaru* is probably derived from the French *loup-garou*, or werewolf.

Locality: Twenty miles south of New Orleans on Hwy 45, west on Hwy 301 to its end; then one quarter mile through cane field west of the village of Lafitte on the bank of a body of water called The Pen (Fig. 59).

Diagnosis: Probably stood upwards of 7'6" and weighed some 400 pounds; large canine teeth, rectangular orbits, lower jaw deep with receding chin; Distal ends of femur as wide antero-posterior as transversely, usually indicative of power-strove running but at the expense of maneuverability.

Discussion: The creature wore a quartz crystal wrapped with copper wire and attached to a length of old beaded chain, of the type used with bath tub stoppers (Fig. 63). The crystal is of the type very common in Arkansas. If this creature collected his crystal in the Ozarks, it is possible that it was he who gave rise to Bigfoot legends. Footprint size is certainly right and this creature is said to have been rather hairy. The only difference is

104

that Bigfoot is said to be shy and retiring and *Rugaru* is rather aggressive and dangerous. T-Jean feels the aggressive behavior reported for *Rugaru* is that of a few individuals retaliating for the usurping of their swamps and that most are quite secretive by nature.

Figure 63 *Close-up of quartz crystal pendant.*

Figure 64 *Skadaria skeleton.*

SKADARIA

he discovery of this creature is perhaps the most fortuitous of the lot. A close friend and colleague at my university, Dr. John Ubelaker, is a Biology Professor specializing in Parasitology. He is interested in all aspects of natural history and has accompanied me on a number of expeditions to Mexico. As a result, he's familiar with most of our prospecting and recovery techniques. When he was heading for Yugoslavia to do a parasite survey of Lake Skadar, I didn't need to remind him to watch for fossil vertebrates. Most of the rest of the story is his.

His crew included three of his own graduate students plus a complement of Yugoslav scientists and students. They navigated the huge, but shallow Lake Skadar, collecting fish and snails and then isolating and identifying their parasites. This involved lots of snorkeling and some wading and netting. The area is a karst region with many caves which occur at all elevations from high on the hillsides overlooking the lake to below water level. Some of the flooded caves appear as dark spots in the gin-clear water. Large numbers of fish congregate in the larger ones and are commercially harvested there.

John told me that often during his leisure time he met people who spoke English at one of the picturesque pubs. He would always ask about vampires, etc. After all, this is the area of many "sightings" of such literary characters. Some would scoff, some would laugh, but some would put on a serious face and tell of some supernatural experience. Curiously, most of the stories were of wolfmen. One old gentleman wearing a Turkish style cap even said that he knew where one was. He was not about to go there but he would draw a map. It seems that some years before his anchor got entangled and he swam down to work it loose. It was in one of the dark holes (a submerged cave). Only a few feet below the surface in what must have been a small room off the entrance of the main cavern, he told of seeing rubble of large flat stone slabs. On one of these he saw a partial skeleton that had a skull that looks half man and half wolf. John folded the little map and put it in his wallet. A week later they were in that area and he asked one of the Yugoslav students to look at the map. He

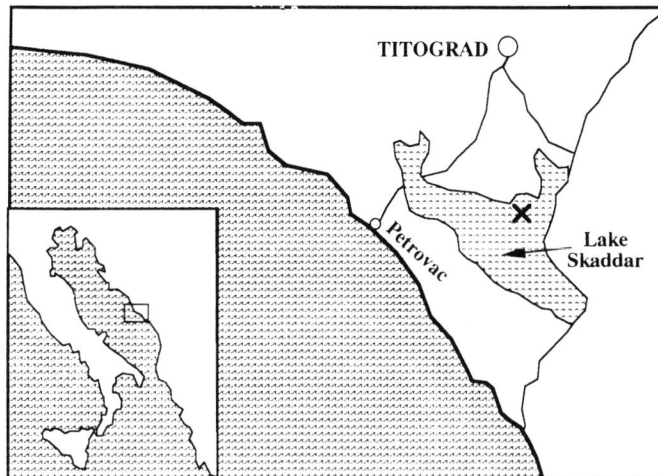

Figure 65 *Skadaria locality.*

immediately knew that "sink" and took John there. The crew snorkeled about looking for the side room. When one of the students called John he swam over and dove into the vestibule. There was a sort of rubble of large flat rocks but it would take considerable time to examine the surface of all of them searching for fossils. He therefore waited until the following day and returned with scuba gear. Most of the slabs were of a dark sandstone but a few had a stiff light colored clay laminated to them. It was in this clay that he found a skull on one slab. The clay was too soft to maintain its integrity without the sandstone but it did cling to the dark stone tenaciously. John used the boom on the boat to raise the block. He covered it with a wet blanket and went back down to see if he could find the adjacent block with the rest of the skeleton. They could find no more bone but one slab had most of the clay missing and there appeared to be parts of a sword buried in the dark level. This too was brought up and the remaining clay removed exposing a beautiful sword handle and a broken bronze sword blade. There were also dog, or wolf tracks in the dark sandstone, one quite huge. John knows anatomy, and this clearly was no ordinary skeleton.

After returning to the research station, the specimen was discussed and it was decided that John could ship the rocks to Texas in exchange for leaving his equipment with the institute. This was John's plan anyway.

To see what else the old fellow in the Turkish cap knew, he returned to the pub and asked him what he thought the skeleton was. The old man was very adamant that it was a skeleton of a wolfman. His dad had told him many stories of such creatures living in the caves below the old Roman ruins and he figured this one got trapped when the dam was built. The dam was built in

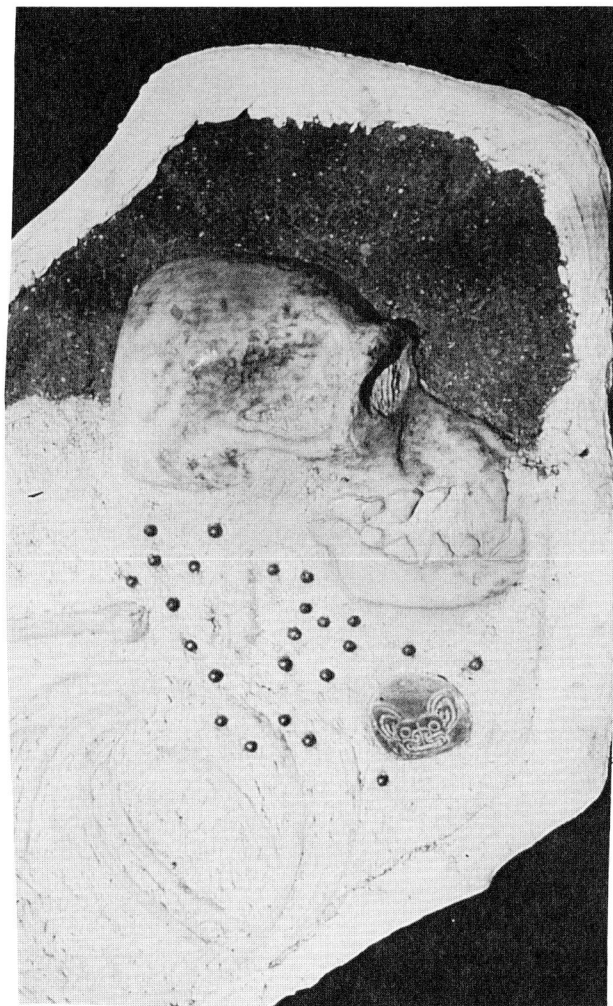

Figure 66 *Close-up of Skadaria skull.*

108

Albania about the turn of the century backing water far into Montenegro. When John brought the blocks to our preparatory laboratory on a large four wheel dolly we opened the one with the sword first. With minimal use of the airscribe we cleaned up the sword handle (Fig. 67). It appears to be made of ivory with the guard made of bronze. The main portion of the blade, which is also bronze is associated with the handle although it is broken off at both ends. The sediment is organic sandstone with a few land snail shells, all of terrestrial species (Helix pomatia). The snail shells in the clinging clay, however, are all aquatic (Melanoides) and the clay is of a type deposited in quiet water. I feel sure the transition represents a rise in water level flooding the cave.

We then opened the other block and the dark organic sandstone was completely covered with the clay lens. It did indeed have a skull exposed and it was a simple matter to bring it into complete relief. It has the cranium of primitive man but the muzzle and dentition were clearly that of a carnivore (Fig. 66). We removed more of the clay and exposed the cervical (neck) vertebrae and then some ribs. It was clear that the lower part of the skeleton would be on the next slab. John was certain that the adjacent slab was not there and probably had fallen off into the depths of the cave. We cleaned off all the clay we could and exposed the individual's right arm in complete articulation and it is 100% human. There also is a bronze medallion embossed with a stylized head of what I'd call a hyena. A number of copper beads are associated. The creature clearly was not just a wild beast. Whether or not the sword belonged to this creature cannot be proven. In fact, the bones being associated with the clay lens and the sword with the sandstone level, one cannot be sure that the two are even contemporary. There are a few human finger bones embedded in the dark

sandstone and they are of a different preservation than that of the skull and probably don't belong to the same individual. I suspect, however, that the creature lay on the dark sand floor and then was covered by water borne clay later. In any case, the age difference between the two levels is not great. The lower body and legs of the creature are unknown. There are three tracks of a huge carnivore, two in the sandstone lens of the skeleton block, and one on the sword block. These are larger than any wolf prints I've ever seen. There are 27 square centimeters of foot surface on these and that is exactly the number in a male size ten human footprint. I feel that this creature not only shared skull features between man and carnivore but the hind limbs as well. An interesting aspect is the minutiae of the dentition. It is not wolf-like, but is like that of a hyena. If one were to see such a creature in the flesh, I'm sure half-wolf and half-man would be the first impression, especially if they were familiar with wolves and not hyenas. The name wolfman, therefore may be a misnomer. I shall withhold this proposal, however because we cannot be sure that this is the creature men have called wolfman. Personally, I believe that this form is what has been called werewolf or wolfman but it serves no purpose to debate the subject. For this reason, the name I'm proposing does not reflect my beliefs concerning its relationships or origins.

Skadaria ubelakeri, new genus and species
Figs. 64, 66

Type specimen: LU 66297 Skull and jaws; proximal vertebral column to pelvic; both arms.

Diagnosis: Hominoid with the cranium of a primitive human and the dentition of a hyena (Fig. 66). The evidence is that the legs and feet probably were also those of a hyena.

Type locality: From submerged cave in the north west end of Lake Skadar in southern Yugoslavia near the city of Titograd (Fig. 65).

Etymology: *Skadaria* (from Lake Skadar) + *ubelakeri*, named for Dr. John Ubelaker, lifelong natural historian.

Discussion: The dark organic sandstone apparently was the cave floor when it was dry and, I suspect, a living surface of the creature. It includes tracks of what I believe to be the same form, if not the same individual, as well as tracks of normal size for a large dog or a wolf (or hyena). They could represent young of *Skadaria* or it could mean that *Skadaria* lived in association with wild animals.

The ivory handle sword (Fig. 67) is not unlike Middle Eastern swords of the Middle Ages but it is not certain whether it belonged to Skadaria, was a trophy of his, or just belonged to an earlier cave visitor. In the same dark sediments are a few hand and finger bones indistinguishable from those of humans. They are dark in color due to the organic make up of the sediments.

In 1901 a low dam was built in Albania that backed water far into Montenegro (this part of Yugoslavia) enlarging Lake Skadar. Many of these caves were filled with water at that time, and it is not out of the question that our example was trapped in his cave then.

Whether or not the sword belonged to Skadaria, the necklace and amulet most certainly did. Therefore, this was not simply a wild beast as he adorned himself. Considering the amulet motif, a stylized hyena, he may have even crafted the amulet himself. Such a creature might appear as a wolfman but his relationships certainly lay closer to hyenas.

Whether or not this is what initiated stories of werewolves, we may never know. 19th and 20th century literature about werewolves usually describe transformations from a normal human into a

Figure 67 *Skadaria's sword.*

scribe transformations from a normal human into a wolfman and back again when he died. Obviously this doesn't hold true for our specimen. I fear any additional information on the life history of *Skadaria* must await additional specimens.

After a lecture I gave on *Skadaria* in Montreal, Quebec, I was approached by Patricia Brady, a reporter for TV Station KCLD.

"I interviewed a lady who teaches Art History at the community college here about her encounters with wolfmen in Yugoslavia. In fact I think it was on the shores of Lake Skadar. I still have the interview tapes. Would you be interested in seeing them?"

"I most certainly would!" I said, admiring the reporter's personality.

That evening after meeting for dinner at the designated Crepe Shop, we made our way to the TV Station. There she produced the tape and we settled down in front of a TV. The transcribed dialogue is as follows:

P. "I'm talking today with Professor Yovona Spalatin whose native land is Yugoslavia. May I call you Yovana?"

Y. "You surely may Patricia."

P. "Professor Spalatin says she has had encounters with wolfmen back home in Yugoslavia. Yovana, would you tell something about these encounters?"

Y. "Well I actually only saw them one time. It was many years ago and my boyfriend, Slavko Skoko, and I were picnicing in an old Roman ruin on a hill overlooking Lake Skadar that forms the border with Albania. We heard strange noises and peeked through the ruins toward the lake and saw these two creatures sitting facing each other, one on a rock and one on a log. Each had a fish and they were eating them raw, scales and all. The inclinations of their voices sounded like they were having a conversation but we could understand nothing. It may have been a language unknown to us or it may just have been their guttural growling voices. Suddenly one held his head high and sniffed the air. He then looked straight at us, and we froze. It was terrifying. They were so large and unusual looking. Then they both stood upright and walked slowly toward the lake taking huge strides. Just before and after they disappeared among the boulders on the beach they produced the strangest laugh.

P. "You never saw them again?"

Y. "I didn't return for over a year but finally I became so curious I went back almost hoping to see them again. After all, they showed no malice towards us. I didn't see them again but several times I heard that strange laugh. Sometimes far away and sometimes quite close.

P. "I'll bet that made you very uncomfortable."

Y. "Not really. I was intrigued that such strange creatures exist and I had no reason to suspect they would harm me.

P. Could you tell us more about their appearance?"

Y. " Well, their upper bodies were quite manlike but rather hairy. When they walked away we could see that their legs were more like those of wolves even though they were walking upright like men. The face was quite wolflike with large fangs protruding. The muzzle was rather broad, however, and the ears were larger than those of wolves and dogs."

P. "Ears larger than those of wolves?"

Y. "Yes."

When the taped interview was finished, we sat in silence for a minute and then Ms. Brady spoke. "Does anything we heard refute or support your conclusions about the beast?"

"As a matter of fact there are two possible areas of support. The broad muzzle and ears larger than those of wolves certainly could reflect the proposed hyena relationships. The other intriguing thing is her mention of the strange laughter. I know a lady, Dr. Bonnie Jacobs, a paleobotanist who lived and worked in Kenya for several years. She can mimic the laughter of a hyena well enough to fool hyenas. I wonder if we could arrange for Dr. Jacobs to perform for Prof. Sparatin?"

The following day Ms. Brady arranged with Prof. Sparatin for us to have a conference call at 5:00 PM that afternoon. I then called Dr. Jacobs and we set it up. With Brady recording everything, the call was made and Dr. Jacobs did her hyena laugh. Even before she was finished Prof. Sparatin broke in, " My god that's it. . . but how could you know?"

I was invited to a reunion of the Knight family near Goldthwaite, Texas. The head of that family was my late Uncle Ed Knight, for whom I had greatest affection and respect. He had done an excellent job passing his values onto his many descendants and I like them all. After a humongus lunch of barbecued brisket, fried chicken, pinto beans, potato salad, iced tea, and peach cobbler, everyone showed their snapshots of grandchildren, pets, fishing boats, etc. Eventually, I found myself in a one on one discussion with a second cousin, one Janetha Woodard. At some point, my longtime interest in squirrels came out and this reminded Janetha of something I found most interesting. When she returned to Mills County for semi-retirement, she purchased a small ranch across the road from her childhood home. Her two brothers, Charles Ed and Carlos decided to clear out a number of dead mesquite trees from the pasture in back of her new house, partially to improve the view and partially to furnish her with firewood. The largest of these was very close to maximum size for a mesquite and it was decided to keep a couple sections of the trunk for possible picnic table pedestals. The trunk was hollow and in the bottom was a nest containing the skeleton of a squirrel. Janetha thought that interesting enough to put the section in the storage shed. She said it was still there.

"Would that be of interest to a squirrel enthusiast?" she asked.

"I'd like to see it. You know some years ago some fossil skeletons of small reptiles were found in the hollows of very ancient petrified trees in Nova Scotia. Your specimen would make a good example to use in a museum exhibit to demonstrate their origin."

Janetha said that she had to stay and help clean up but if I wanted to drop by her house on the way back to Ladonia and look at it, it was in the shed in the back yard.

She added,"Its quite heavy but if you can load it by yourself, its yours".

When I looked into the hollow stump, I could

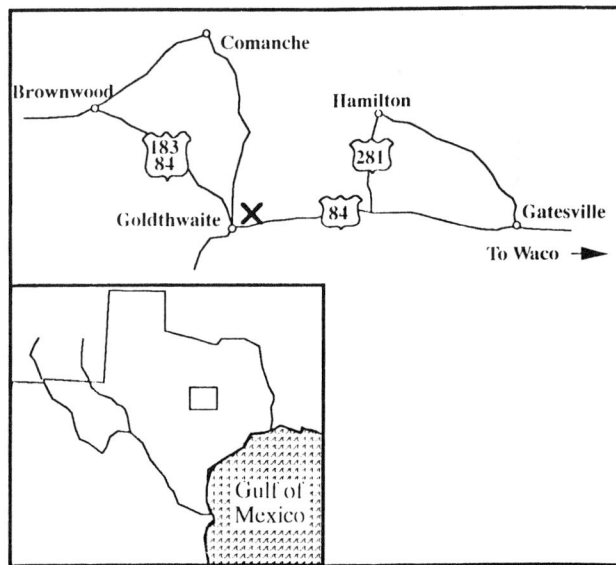

Figure 69 *Texas Gnome locality.*

113

see the better part of a squirrel skeleton mixed with leaves. I couldn't lift the stump but with the help of a couple short 2 x 8's in the shed with which I made a ramp, I managed to slide it into the van.

Back at the lab I unloaded and examined the stump more closely. There were indeed bones of a squirrel but there was also a tibia that was very hominid looking. I decided to remove the nest containing the squirrel bones to see what other surprises the log might hold. In the very bottom of the packed, but loose leaves I could see that leaf fragments had mixed with a sort of sawdust from boring insects and some sap dating to when the tree was alive had cemented the whole thing together. It was soft, however, and easy to remove. As I began scratching the remaining bones into relief, I could see that I had another fringe homonoid.

Homo knighti, new species
Fig. 68

Holotype: Complete skeleton of a male individual that would have stood about fourteen inches tall.

Diagnosis: Small size (about twelve inches); otherwise quite like modern man.

Specimen: LU 63498, Complete skeleton.

Description: It is a skeleton is about the size of the *Cliff End Fairies*, but the head is larger. The sternum is not ossified as in the flying fairies and the fibula is present, unlike the fairies. The limbs are short relative to the body size when compared to a modern human skeleton. I can't help but think of it as a *New World Gnome*.

Locality: Large mesquite tree that grew on the Janetha Woodard Ranch eight miles east of Goldthwaithe, Texas on Highway 84 (Fig. 69).

Etymology: Named after my late Uncle Ed Knight, Mills County, Texas Pioneer and master of ethics, wit, and wisdom.

Discussion: Our little Texas gnome is less than one hundred and twenty years old. Although badly deteriorated, there are remnants of clothing not unlike that of many rural residents today. There are remains of his tiny, hand-made, leather shoes, which are of a style that allows tightening with a draw string without the need of eyelets, brads, or hooks. The trousers were made of jean material, his shirt is a light denim and there are the remains of a straw hat not unlike those worn by my farming relatives when I was a lad.

A most interesting and important object associated is a German coin belt buckle. The date (1877) certainly gives a maximum date for the death of our little "gnome" and strongly hints that his kind came with the some of the many German immigrants to Texas during late 19th Century. Of particular interest, however, is a spiral etched into the reverse side so small that it takes magnification to see. Surely, it refers to his *Eunano* ancestry. I feel this supports the hypothesis that after the *Eunano* reached northern Europe with the Celts (*DeSanders Gnome*) and Ireland with the Beaker People (*Boyne River Leprechaun*), they began an evolutionary downsizing.

Although hollow, the tree was alive when our little "gnome" was living there, Overgrowth has almost obscured a piece of commercial wire-glass that had been installed as a window. No door remains but rusty hinges testify to the presence of one. The door may have been ripped away when the chain saw hit it. There is a stairway carved from the wood that spirals around in such a way as to be certain that there were additional floors of living space higher in the hollow tree. In fact, for one so small, the hollow tree must have made a relatively safe and comfortable home.

I find it fascinating that such creatures could live in our midst without being detected. I spent considerable time tramping through the fields and

woods of these parts as a youngster, as did my
many cousins, and never had a hint that the likes of
gnomes were roaming the same area. It conjures up
a scenario of the rural gnomes leaving the farms
and small towns to go to the city, like most of the
human population. Are these little people sharing
our urban space too? Somehow, I hope so.

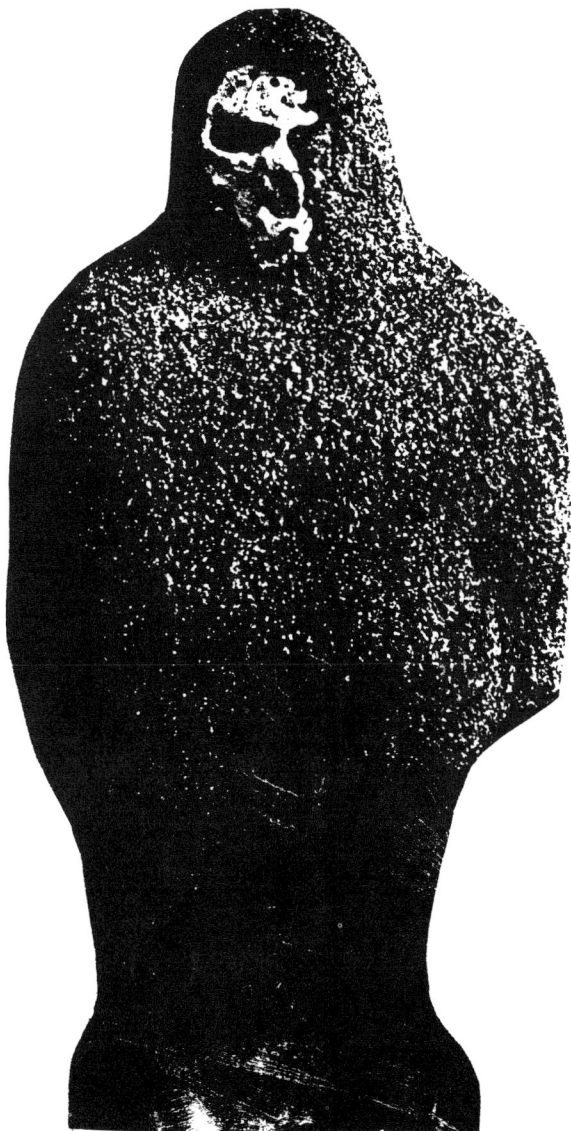

Figure 70 *Stone Tiki.*

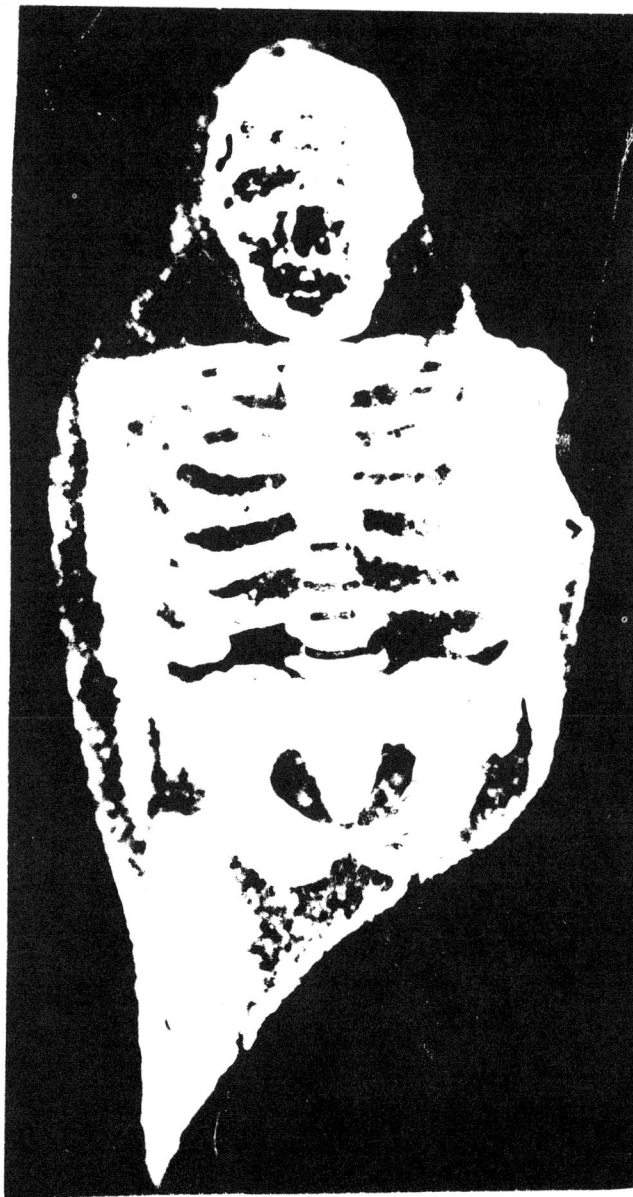

Figure 71 *X-ray of Tiki.*

116

TIKI

In the summer of 1991 my wife, Juliana, had the happy occasion to be assistant to Dr. Victoria Lockwood, Cultural Anthropologist, on a study of Tahitian women. They visited five islands, one of which could only be reached by boat. This was the most primitive of the group and when they arrived she remembered my request. I had asked her to inquire about local myths of fringe humanoids, gods, demons, etc. When asked, the people always told about the *Tiki*. *Tiki* are carved of stone or wood and variously represent gods of this and that, or sometimes ancestors, either individually or collectively. Some of these stone images are a few inches tall but often they are up to four or five feet tall. They universally appear as dwarfs with the head and body outsized for the short legs. When she reached the island of Raivavae, the answer was always relating to a single *Tiki*, which was in a rather inaccessible area that no one visited. The main reason no one visited the site was that when a man tried to collect the large *Tiki* and knocked it from its stone perch, breaking its legs off, the man died the following day. Two other deaths were attributed to people trying to collect the specimen. If they were trying to discourage Juliana from visiting this awesome *Tiki*, they could have saved their breath. The more she heard, the more certain she became. At last she found a guide for a fee and discovered it wasn't nearly as inaccessible as she had been led to believe. In fact, it was just a short walk from a shell road. She knew the apprehension was real, however, when her guide insisted she pay him at the entrance to a path he said would lead to the carving and then fled.

She found the place beautiful, quiet and very "special." It was completely shaded by copious mangrove growth and stones were placed to form line patterns and altars called Maraie. Originally, the *Tiki* had places of honor on these altars but most have been collected and sold to museums and wealthy individuals. When she found the "statue" it was laying on its side in a small ravine behind the Maraie with a miniature waterfall pouring directly onto it. It seemed to be carved rust colored stone and like the smaller ones she had seen, rather like a fat dwarf. As she examined it closer she was startled to see that part of the head was broken and weathered exposing a skull. How could the skull get inside the stone carving? Was the stone once flesh? This seemed the best possibility, but how?

In any case, she decided to see if it was possible to bring it back to me. It weighed several hundred pounds and she knew there was no way she could get locals to help. In fact, when she remembered the demise of three others who tried to move the statue, she sat down and had a long talk with *Tiki*. She told him of the wonders of the western world and of the other deities he could be with. She furthermore promised to return him to his home at the slightest signal from him. When she felt she had his approval she set to finding a crew and making whatever arrangements with the officials. The officials were willing for her to have a go at it by considering it a long term loan and asking

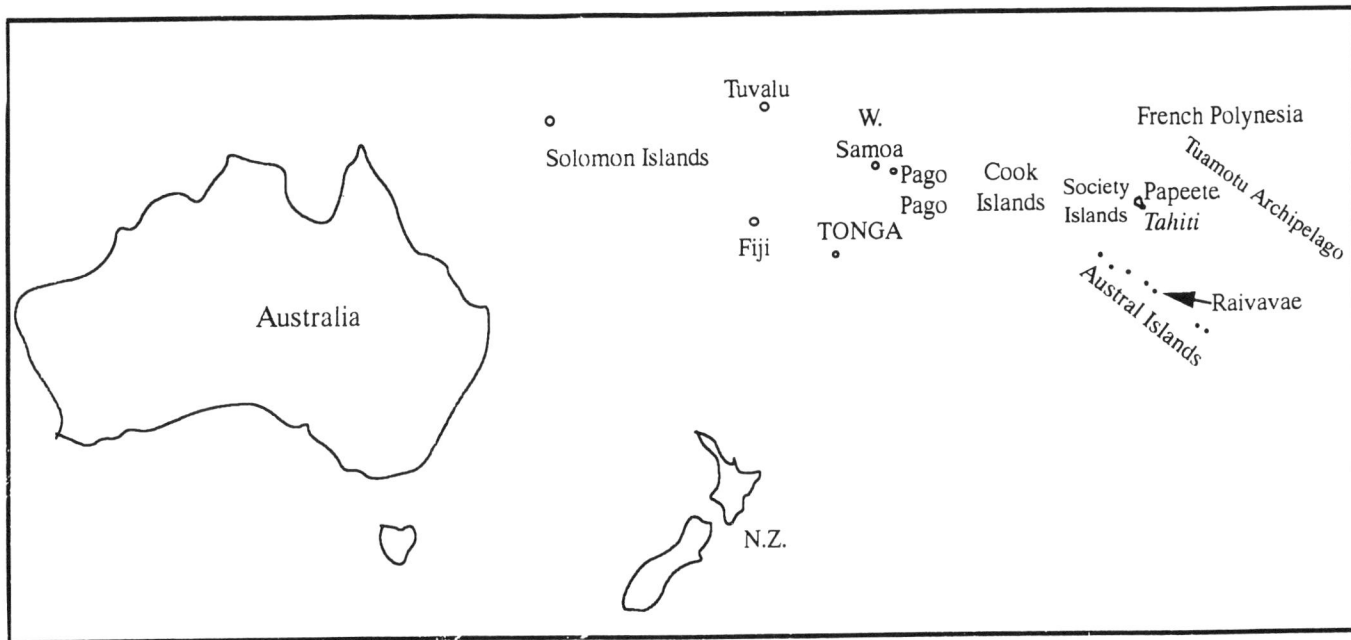

Figure 72 *Tiki locality.*

proper acknowledgement of their cooperation. Their cooperation did not extend to physical help, however, and Juliana had the distinct feeling that they too were a little apprehensive of moving the cursed *Tiki.* Juliana is very persuasive, however, and it was not long before she had recruited a crew made up of a French doctor who had made the island his home for many years, his wife, and two tourists anxious to be a part of an archeological recovery. The doctor had a small pickup and off they went. When they arrived, she renegotiated her deal with *Tiki* and the work began. Fortunately, the trip to the truck was downhill and they were able to roll it directly into the pickup. Before turning it over to the craters, she wisely wrapped the specimen with rags, partially to protect its surface, but mainly to hide the fact that it has a skeleton inside.

When Juliana called me, I knew she would not kid me about such a thing, but I still thought that she was mistaken somehow. Perhaps the stone had a sort of weathered patina and the break exposed the different colored core. I was as surprised when the specimen arrived three months later, as if she had not even mentioned the skeleton. There was no doubt about it— the skull was in place. I took the specimen to the medical school where a friend took several X-rays. Not only is the skull in place but there is a complete skeleton inside— unique in my knowledge of humanoid creatures. A new name is certainly justified.

Tiki holcombi, new genus and species
Figs. 70, 71

Locality: Northwest corner of the Tahitian

118

Island of Raivavae, South Pacific (Fig. 72).

Diagnosis: Skull and body larger than most modern men but legs very short. Orbits rectangular, not unlike a gorilla but the muzzle and inflated frontals are more like modern man.

Etymology: *Tiki* is the name used by many Polynesians for similar stone "statues." The specific name *holcombi* is in honor of Bobby Holcomb, the artist and folk singer so beloved by Tahitians.

Discussion: X-rays and sonograms have demonstrated that the skeleton is in complete articulation (Fig. 71), save of course, the missing leg. The most puzzling question is how did the skeleton get into the rock? Could there have been a volcanic ash mold of the body like the ones at Pompeii and like that of the Japanese *Oni*, and later filled with sand? I still have found no one who can offer a reasonable explanation of how the flesh could have turned to rock other than introducing the individual to *Medusa*. One suggestion was that the sculptor intuitively knew where the skeleton was in a larger rock unit and carved the statue to coincide. The why and how of this introduces just as many questions.

WHITE BUFFALO SPIRIT

hen archaeologists from the Museum of the Great Plains in Lawton, Oklahoma, discovered the fossil remains of an Ice Age Mammoth, they contacted a crew of Texans who worked on Ice Age problems. Dr. Claude Albritton (geologist), Drs. Don Allen and Elmer Cheatum (conchologists), and I answered the call. By the time we arrived, flint spear points had been found in the mammoth's rib cage, increasing the probability of a symposium on the ancient kill site. One of the museum people, geologist Frank Chapibitty, is full blood Comanche Indian and lots of fun. He is also a wealth of knowledge concerning Indian lore and history and we all were constantly asking him questions as we excavated. The conversation never let up as we worked and at some point Frank was telling us some of the lore surrounding the *White Buffalo Spirit*. Laughingly, he told us that there was an antique/junk dealer who offered to sell the Museum some footprints of a *White Buffalo*.

I countered, "It's hard enough to tell a footprint is a buffalo from that of a cow. How in the name of the Great Spirit could one identify the track of a WHITE buffalo"?

Frank was quick to admit that he too was doubtful but said, "Old Cactus Jack, owner of an antique/junk establishment, is adamant. His story is that it was brought in by a old drunk who said his uncle stole the piece from a Museum. Even Cactus Jack was skeptical but thought it would be a good crowd pleaser."

"Frank, I have an interest in fossil footprints. I'd like to see this spirit buffalo track." I asked, "Is it still available?"

"We can go see Saturday if you like. Cactus Jack's Store is near the town of Apache."

That Saturday after lunch, Frank and I took one of the pickups and drove to Apache. Old Jack had the preserved footprint displayed in an old TV set. . . guts removed and lights installed, allowing the visitor to peep through the glass and see it without touching it. I chuckled at his ingenuity but wanted to examine it more closely. Frank arranged this by making fantastic claims of my being a famous scientist. The small block of red clay was very professionally collected and preserved. A broken arrow is also preserved laying in such a way as to suggest it was broken by the buffalo's foot. When I asked Jack what made him think it was a Spirit Buffalo that made the tracks, he pointed to a tattered letter. The writing was faded and difficult to read.

"Just tell me what it says," I requested.

"The letter is from Montana and is dated 1824. It was written by a buffalo hunter named Harold Price. It's to his nephew, telling him where to find the piece. It says that he should keep the track and that any experienced Medicine Man can authenticate the tracks as being made by a *Spirit Buffalo* (usually thought to be white). Obviously Price's nephew recovered the piece but we know nothing of its history until the drunk walked in here to sell it."

I have a very good friend , one Dr. Joleta

Figure 73 *Natural light photograph of Spirit Buffalo tracks.*

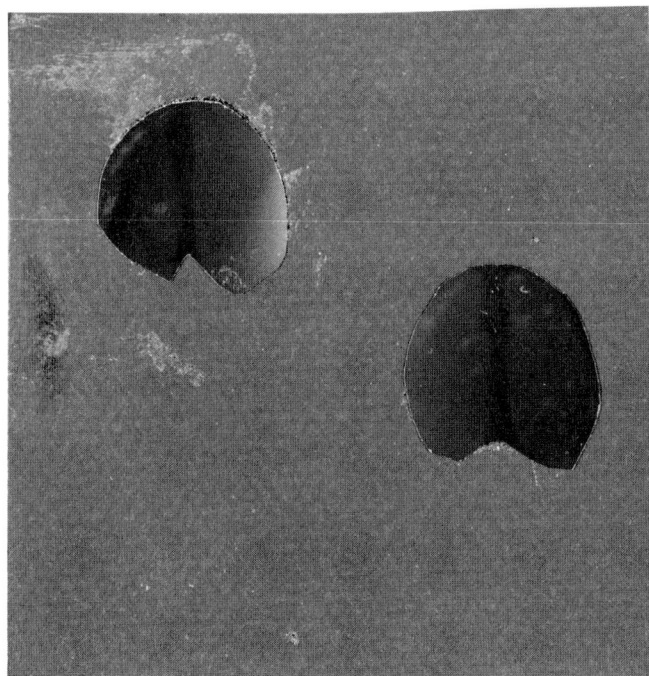

Figure 74 *Black light photograph of same tracks.*

Bishop, who is very interested in the American Indian culture and I could see a Christmas present that she could not guess in a thousand years. I won't tell what I paid for the piece, lest some of you come to me with bridges for sale. Frank thought I was crazy too, but just in case it was as advertised, I knew it would be appreciated and respected by Joleta. I never regretted the purchase.

Years later I had some of the fringe hominoid fossils scattered around the lab getting ready to crate them for an exhibition when a graduate student walked in and turned off the lights. My first reaction was a loud complaint but then I saw a beautiful reddish fluorescence. It was a rock sample she had collected in Costa Rica. With the black light still on, I turned and saw a greenish fluorescence coming from one of my specimens. It proved to be the tracks of *Skadaria*, the "Wolfman" from Yugoslavia. I could think of no reason the sediment should fluoresce just where the creature stepped. The smaller wolf-like tracks in the same slab were not fluorescent and these I presume to be tracks of normal wolves. Next, I tested the tracks of the dancing Duendes of Mexico and they fluoresce red. That night I took a portable shortwave black light to Joleta's place and found that the *Spirit Buffalo* tracks give off a beautiful blue fluorescence (Fig. 74). Apparently, there is some residue left by the feet of mythical creatures that is resistant and reacts to black light. This new tool will have numerous uses for research on mythology and its creatures. Prospecting at night with the black light, we have already found modern footprints of *Leprechauns* just outside Cambridge, Mass. and *Fairies* in Scotland.

One Friday afternoon at our weekly pub brainstorming session, I brought the subject up to see if anyone had any ideas concerning the mechanism of the fluorescence. Here I present a condensed

Figure 75 *Close-up of arrowhead.*

123

Figure 76 *Close-up of feather impression.*

transcription of some of the discussion.

Slaughter: "Today I would like to have your whys and hows concerning the demonstrated fluorescence of modern and fossil footprints of mythical creatures." I then recounted what we had discovered and asked, "What do you think, John?"

Dr. John Ubelaker, Biologist: "Some common life fluids fluoresce. For example, the sap of the Mesquite Tree fluoresces a brilliant yellow. Perhaps some body oils of these creatures do the same. However, it does seem that walking and leaving some behind with each step would deplete the supply very quickly."

After reflecting briefly, John added, "Unless, of course, sources of the residue are glans associated with the feet, as with many forms of mammalian odor."

Dr.Joleta Bishop, Folklorist: "According to Joseph Campbell, the universe viewed by the physical eye alone is but an array of light reflecting shapes. . . They are not self-luminous. They are only visible by daylight and to the daylight mind. . . By night, however, when the sun has set, the mind turns inward. . . (things) change into something rich and strange. . . forms beheld are self-luminous and in definition ambiguous, unsubstantial yet insuppressibly affective. Herein may lay the reason behind Price's statement that any good Medicine Man could authenticate the tracks as being of the Spirit Buffalo. I think Campbell did not mean that the truth could only be seen at night, but rather the truth cannot be seen by the eye alone. Moreover, I doubt that the Medicine Men see ultraviolet fluorescence better than anyone else. I suspect he sees the truth because he is in tune with the Spirit Buffalo more acutely than other men and "sees" the tracks with the eye, plus some other sense. The black light fluorescence is simply a happenstance side effect of the essence."

Slaughter: "That makes sense. The word essence may be critical. The usual definition is that essence includes those properties necessary for something to belong to its species. A creature's DNA is certainly essence, by definition, but the residual odor left behind by a mammal in its footsteps is also essence since a trailing hound dog knows the species that made the footprint. Perhaps the fluorescence is the visual equivalent of the scent the trailing hound follows. If so, perhaps the code can be broken and we can learn which mythical creature is responsible for fluorescing footprints."

In any case, the fact that the fluorescence seems limited to the footprints of mythical creatures is intriguing. I intend to test prints of as many living animals as possible and will certainly take my portable black light wherever I travel, seeking prints of other mythical creatures. Perhaps someday we can assemble a book of color shades of each creature.

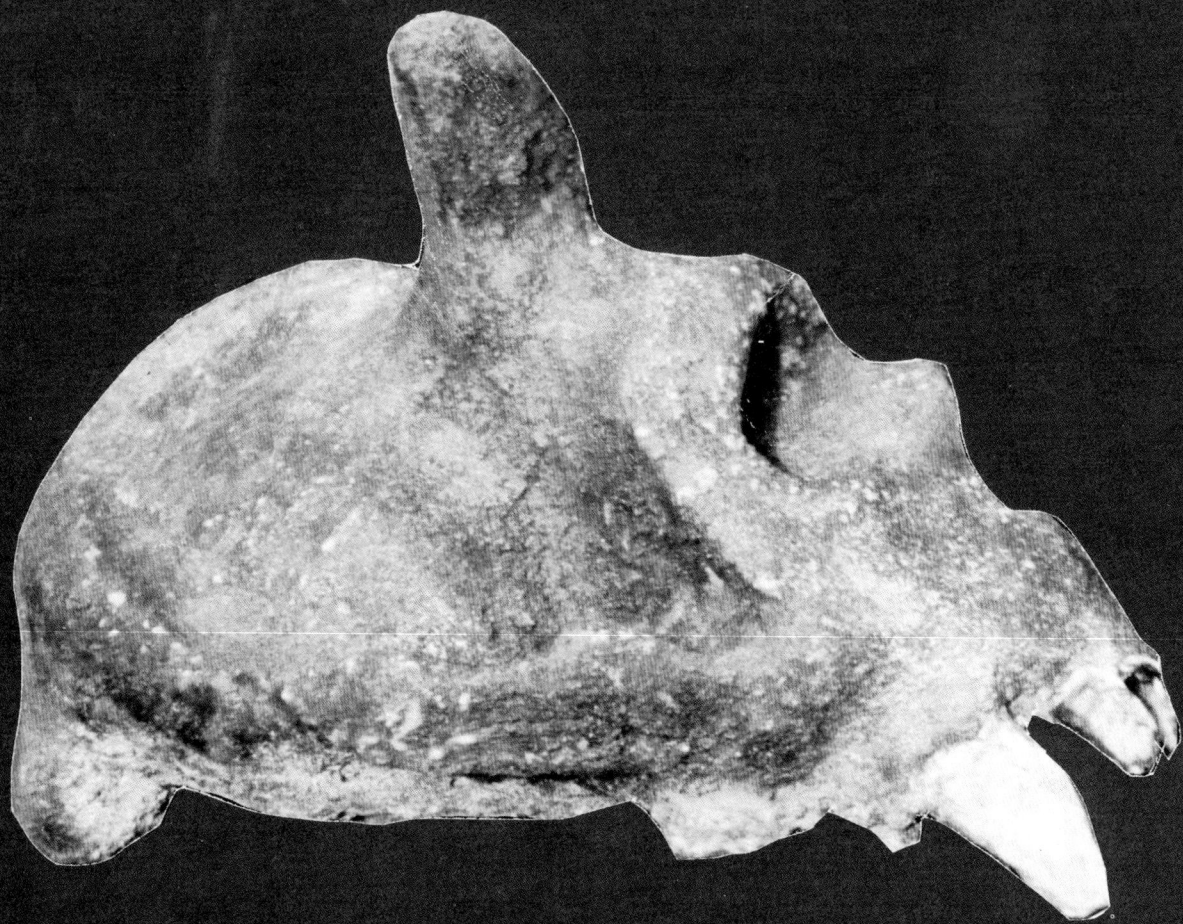

he second day after my wedding, my French Canadian wife and I took off for Montreal, Quebec, on the first leg of our journey to meet her parents. They live, and Juliana was raised, in Roberval, a small town on the shores of twenty mile long Lac St. Jean, three hundred miles north of Montreal. I still remember the hospitality and smiling faces like it was yesterday. One evening a neighbor invited the whole Bernier Clan and myself over to reduce their larder of home-made wine. Juliana's dad, Philippe, was a slight, but handsome man, forever cracking jokes. After a few cups of wine there was a glow upon the crowd and Philippe was singing and playing the accordion with gusto. Juliana would whisper the translation of the songs to me. When one song began, she looked puzzled and turned to me saying she had never heard this one. Paraphrasing, she began:

"The drought of the fifties was killing my lake. I could see no water between me and Ile aux Couleuvres (an island in view of Roberval). I decided to walk the trip I'd made so often by boat and I put on some old cross-country skis and began. I was embarrassed for my race when I saw beer cans and wine bottles mixed with the fish skeletons and beautiful clam shells. When I saw a piece of bone protruding from the mud, I dug, and dug, and dug. Out came the head of a beast. Horns on the skull of a bear-man."

Juliana didn't catch the rest of the verse and Philippe moved quickly into another song. The group was far too jolly to get into any serious discussion, so I waited until the next afternoon to locate Philippe to ask about the origin of the song. Again translated from French by Juliana:

"Its true. I did find the skull of a beast in the mud of the shrinking Lac St. Jean. It had straight flat horns and huge protruding tusks (indicating teeth with his index fingers)."

"What became of the skull?" I inquired.

"When I showed it to Charlotte, she said it was an evil thing and that I was to hasten to bury it far away from the house and so it was done."

"Do you think its still there?" I inquired.

"I don't see why not. Would you like to see it?"

"Mais oui."

Armed only with a small folding trenching tool, we took off, first by car and then by foot.

"I chose this place because the soil is easy to dig," he told us as we walked.

Half expecting the mysterious skull not to be there, I was pleasantly surprised when we arrived and Philippe pointed to a flat piece of bone sticking out of the sandy soil. Within minutes he was holding the strange looking skull high over his head and smiling that infectious smile. It was fairly well preserved although some was broken off. The missing pieces were visible in the hole however, so I recovered them for future reconstruction. If it were not for the circumstances, I would have been very suspicious, thinking someone had made a composite skull. Close examination, however, revealed no areas of joining of different bones. The cranium most certainly looks like that of an ape or

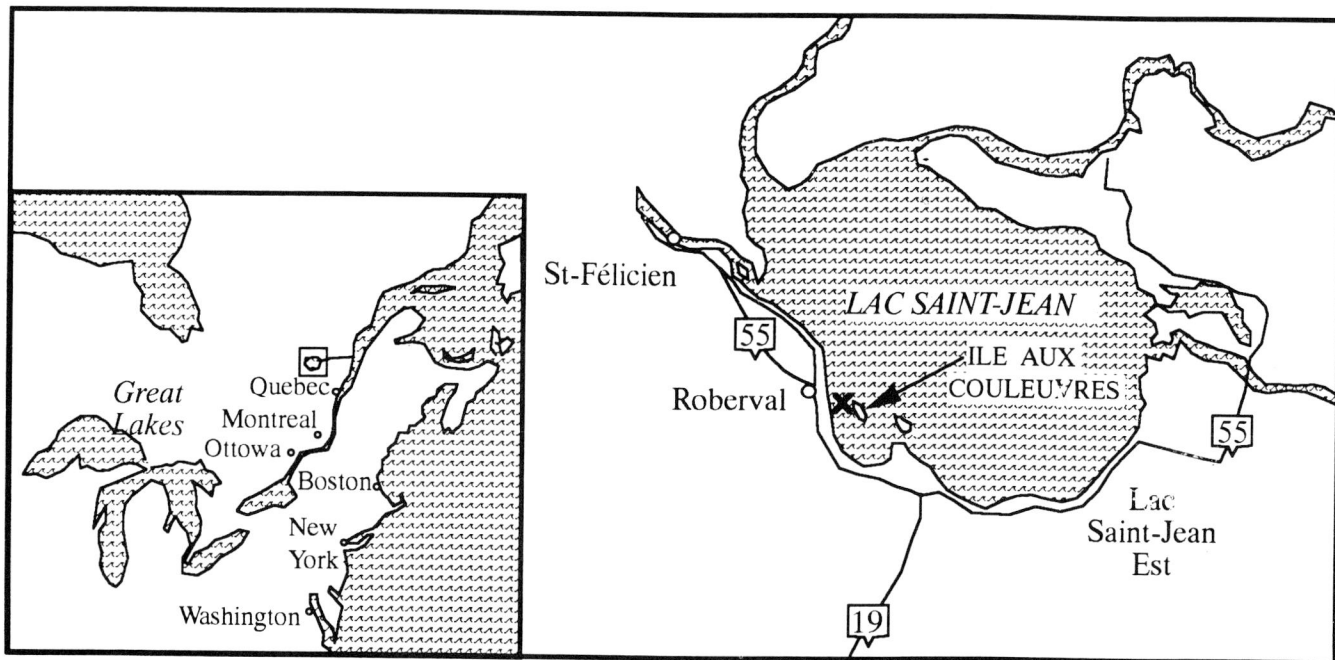

Figure 77 *Map showing approximate area of the lake where the skull of a supposed Windigo was found.*

primitive man, but primates have only two incisors in each quadrant of the jaw and there are three carnivore-like incisors in this specimen. The orbits are closed behind in primate fashion but the single large molar is very like that of a bear. The horn cores have no burr at the base as those of bison, cow, goat, etc. Such horn cores are present in only two types of mammals I know of; the American Pronghorn Antelope, and the Giraffe. Such a combination of features is certainly unknown to me.

"What do you think it is?" I asked Philippe.

"An old Montagnais Indian who lives at Pointe Bleue told me it was a *Windigo*, a spirit that plagued his people as far into the distant past as anyone can remember," Philippe said with his eyes enlarged and intense.

When we took the skull back to Juliana's childhood home, her mother, Charlotte, met us at the door telling us in no uncertain terms that we were not coming in the house until we had divested ourselves of the skull. We took it to the shed out back and constructed a box to fit the skull with enough soft packing to assure its safe arrival back at the University. Its description follows:

Windigo bernieri new genus and species

Fig. 78

Diagnosis: Totally unique skull with flat barrel horns and the dentition somewhat like a bear. The orbits are closed behind, like a primate, and the eyes are directed straight forward for stereoscopic vision. There is a strong saggital crest on the braincase, indicating powerful jaw closure.

Type locality: From the bottom of Lac St. Jean about half way between the town of Roberval and Ile sux Couleuvres (Fig. 77).

Etymology: *Windigo* is the Indians' vernacular name for the beast + *bernieri* named in honor of Charlotte and Philippe Bernier— Philippe

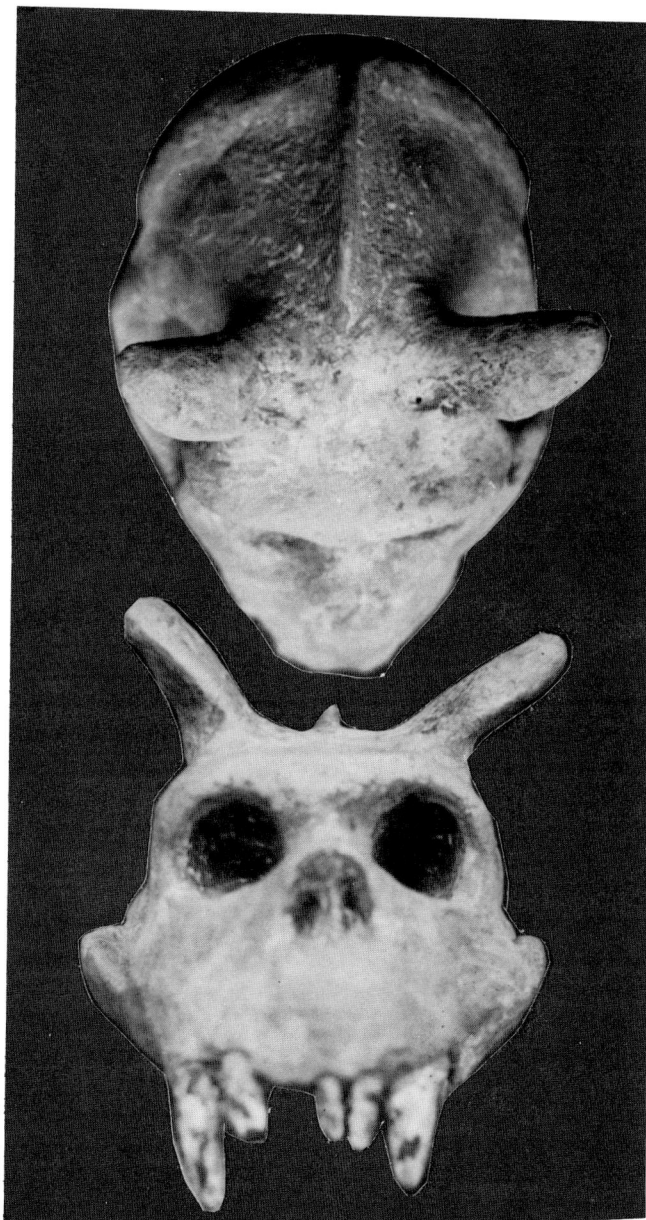

Figure 78 *Front and dorsal views of the Windigo skull.*

129

as the discoverer and Charlotte as the one responsible for the specimen's safe reburial.

Discussion: I didn't learn much concrete about the *Windigo* from interviews with some of the Montagnais Indians. I was told by several that *Windigo* were cannibals. As this skull certainly didn't belong to any race of man, it would be more accurate to say that they ate/eat men. The size according to the stories, varied from taller than a fir tree to the size of a grizzly bear. Our specimen seems to indicate the latter.

The large canine teeth were described as long and catlike. They are pointed, but thick and robust, more like those of a bear. Most agreed that the horns were forked. These horn cores are not forked but the forked horns of Pronghorn Antelope are not reflected in the cores and these cores are flattish and barrels like horns of pronghorns. It was very clear that these Indians had either seen our beast or had heard eye witness accounts of them. None of the Indians interviewed knew anything about the creature's feet. Some believed they were like those of a bear and some believed they were cloven like those of a moose. Some even said they were not unlike those of man, pointing out that this may be the same creature that's called *Sasquatch*, or *Bigfoot*, west of the Rocky mountains. In any case, knowledge of skeletal features other than the skull must await additional specimens.

The position of the occipital condyles indicates he carried his head upright but pitched forward, however.

The range of *Windigo* is said to be roughly that of all Montagnais, Cree, and Algonquian tribes of northern Canada, from the Maritimes of the east to the Rocky Mountains. *Rugaru* is the only other of our fringe hominoids approaching *Windigo's* size. However, *Rugaru* is much more primate-like than *Windigo* and surely the two are not related. It's also interesting that *Sasquatch* is said to range west of the Rockies. Could it be that they are only separated by semantics and are, in fact, the same? Or, perhaps they are mutually exclusive — *Sasquatch* is shy and retiring, whereas *Windigo* is said to be rather aggressive. Also, there is the problem of the horns. I've heard of no suggestion of horns in accounts of human-*Sasquatch* encounters.

Mr. Clifford Moar recently called my wife's attention to an article from the Musee Amerindian of Quebec, Canada. In this, *Windigo* is cast as originally being a protector of the Indians from natural disasters. It was not until the invasion of the Europeans that he became disgusted with the greed of some Indians who killed wildlife for profit instead of need. He then took up the position of a sort of mega-game warden, punishing the polluters and poachers. I find that I much prefer this image to one where he indiscriminately attacks Indians and other woodsmen. I also find it more probable.

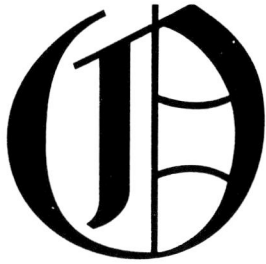

One of the most delightful characters I've known is one Jack Connelly; photographer, musician, race car driver, and humorist. Jack was proud of his Irish heritage, but not nearly so fanatically as his dad. His dad collected books on Irish history and heraldry and made trips to Ireland when he could afford it. It is for his dad, as well as Jack, that I'm so pleased to relate Jack's short discovery story.

Jack was into all fads; fossils and minerals gave way to artifacts, which gave way to coins and other treasures found with the "new" toy, a metal detector. Each time I'd come into his photography shop, he'd have some "new" discovery; either fossil, coin, or historical artifact. If he had lived twice his alloted sixty years, he could not have come up with anything that would have pleased me more than the following.

Not long after the metal detecting craze took over, Jack made a trip to Massachusetts to check out some details of his genealogy for his dad. Naturally he had his metal detector along when he drove into the countryside. Sometime that day he spotted the charred remains of an old house that had completely collapsed many years before (we later found out that the house burned in 1932). He patiently scoured the grounds with his detector getting closer and closer to the rubble of the house itself. As soon as he began to check the ashes of the house, the detector sounded off as if he placed it against a truck. He thought it must be a piece of plumbing pipe, or the like.

He found the head of old corn bin fork and used it like a rake scratching at the charred wood bits, ash, and dirt. Even after he reached the natural surface beneath the house, the detector insisted he dig deeper. Jack continued probing until he heard the telltale "clank". When the object came to light it required no study to know what it was. As corroded as it was, he could clearly see that it was a tiny copper casket (Fig. 79). It is of the type that the lid closes (or opens) in two parts. The lid portion at the head end was missing and the casket was full of dirt and ash. There was a corroded copper or bronze medal of some sort attached to the top. As soon as his brush exposed a portion of a skeleton, Jack called me in Texas. I asked if he could stop by Dallas on his way home to Corpus Christi and he agreed.

I met him at the airport and drove as fast as I thought I could get by with to the University where we have all the proper tools. In no time, had the skeleton exposed and the medal partially cleaned. The medallion attached to the casket lid, turned out to be an Irish coin dated 1928. I think it unlikely that our *Leprechaun* brought the coin with him from Ireland and died the same year. Its much more likely that his lineage goes back somewhat earlier and the coin was acquired later as a keepsake. It was the first coin minted after Ireland gained its independence from England. In any case, it surely brackets the *Leprechaun's* death between 1928 (probably a year or two later) and 1932, when the house under which he was buried burned.

The individual stood about thirteen inches tall and had rather normal limb/trunk length ratios. For that reason I feel it is an American *Leprechaun*, probably belonging to a lineage that accompanied the influx of Irishmen who emigrated to New England in the late 19th Century. Both *Gnomes* and *Leprechauns* downsized from the ancestral *Eunanos*, but the *Leprechauns* maintained normal limb length/trunk size while the limbs became shorter relative to the trunk in the *Gnome* lineage.

I am reluctant to propose a new formal name for this little humanoid since *Homo knighti*, the presumed emigrant German *Gnome* differs only in limb/trunk ratios. Although I believe *Leprechauns* and *Gnomes* independently downsized from *Eunano* stock, *Gnomes* and *Leprechauns* certainly display no more variation than modern subspecies of *Homo sapiens*. I will therefore refer to this important fossil simply as the *Connolly Leprechaun*.

Figure 79 *Connolly Leprechaun.*

Figure 80 *Close-up of Connolly Leprechaun skeleton.*

EUNANO, CROMAGNONS OF THE LITTLE PEOPLE

r. Paul McGrew of the University of Wyoming, was one of the most fun paleontologists I've known. His best buddy for his adult life was Professor Bryan Patterson of the Field Museum of Chicago. During a field conference of the Society of Vertebrate Paleontology which was held in Wyoming, Paul taped several hours of Bryan telling humorous paleontological stories of field work during the thirties and forties. Paul would often bring these tapes to the annual meeting for the paleontology students to listen to at room parties. I finally convinced Paul to allow me to copy the tapes, but only if I would come to Wyoming. The following year I made the trip. After the copying was done, he took me on a several day excursion of the geology and fossil sites of his beloved state.

While riding about, he told me about the Basque herders of Wyoming and Idaho. It seems that young Basque men had been coming to the area under contract as herders. They usually arrived at about 18-20 years of age and "took over" a wagon of an older Basque. They would stay here, living in the gypsy-type wagon for twenty to thirty years and then retire in Spain. The herders lonely life was made somewhat easier by their habit of carving and painting the wagon. Hardly a quarter inch of the wagon, its wheels, and undercarriage was left untouched.

Paul took me to meet one of these characters and to see his magnificent wagon. It was indeed a fabulous museum piece. The Basque herder was also most interesting and was exuberant over his forthcoming retirement, only months away. Since Francisco was from the same area of Spain that is home of the *Eunano*, I questioned him about these CroMagnons of the Little People. He grinned an almost fiendish grin while I was telling him what I knew of the *Eunano*. At last he could stand it no longer and disappeared into the wagon. When he returned he was carrying two wood cylinders that were ornately carved and painted much like the wagon. The wood cylinders were hinged and while watching me intently, he opened one and removed a small humanoid skull which also was ornately carved. He told us that many Basque herders brought the little skulls with them to assure their return to Spain. It seems, according to Francisco, the *Eunano* cremate the bodies of their dead and only save the skulls, which are carved and enclosed in boxes made from the limb of a tree. The *Eunano* did not carve the boxes because they are hidden in trees. The bone appears to have little antiquity and certainly the "casket" is too young to radiocarbon date. I asked Francisco if he thought the skulls were carved by *Eunano* or Basque. He was adamant that they were carved by the *Eunano* themselves although the carvings on the *Eunano* boxes were done by their herder owners. After all, one cannot carve a wagon forever. While most boxed *Eunano* skulls in America were "inherited" by new herders from the retiring herders, like the wagons, he had found one of his himself. His was nearly grown over by the living tree it was lashed to and surely had never been seen by modern Basque other than himself.

I simply had to have one of the skulls to

compare to those from Germany and Ireland, but knew how much they meant to him. Nevertheless, I suggested that I might be able to get a donor to furnish the money to allow him to move his retirement up five or six months, which would mean that he, and his replacement, could start making arrangements to move immediately. I was surprised that he jumped at the opportunity. If he had but one, he told me, he would not sell because the young man replacing him might die before retirement if he didn't have a *Eunano* skull with him. However, he would consider selling the one he found himself to get home early.

I telephoned a anonymous benefactor, who is as interested in fringe hominoids as I, and made the arrangements.

The carving of the *Eunano* skull passed through the surficial bone in many places displaying the bone's spongy interior. The design is interesting and probably symbolic but not particularly well crafted. I would presume it was done by a relative and not a bone carving specialist. Of greatest interest are several spiral designs. This specimen came to me after the *Boyne River Leprechaun*, the *DeSanders Gnome*, the *Texas Gnome*, and the *Connelly Leprechaun*, but it is the key specimen to my hypothesis concerning the origin and evolution of *Leprechauns* and *Gnomes*.

It appears to me that some *Eunano* accompanied the Iberians (Celts) as they began to expand their range from Iberia about 4,000 years ago. Those Celts that made it to Ireland early on were called the Beaker People and the *Eunano* with them evolved into the *Leprechauns*. The *Eunano* accompanying the Celts that came to northern Europe became the *Gnomes*. At that time is is doubtful that individuals of the three groups could be distinguished. After they were separated by the English channel, they went on their own

evolutionary paths and both groups began to downsize. The *Gnomes* maintained the relatively short arms and legs of the *Eunano* but the Leprechauns began to take on the limb/trunk ratios of the Beaker/Celts. By the time of the migration of German *Gnomes* to Texas and the *Leprechauns* to the northeast U.S., their height had dropped from about eighteen inches to twelve or fourteen inches. It's easy to see how the English channel formed a gene flow barrier between the *Eunano* and the *Leprechauns* but the ranges of the *Eunano* and the *Gnomes* must have abutted in Europe for millennia. My guess is the Pyrenees Mountains form an effective barrier between the *Eunano* and the *Gnomes*, but this was briefly breached during the initial Celt/*Eunano* migration. If this is the case, *Leprechauns* and *Gnomes* form a sister group and I doubt that the incipient *Leprechaun (Boyne River)* and the Incipient *Gnome (DeSanders)* could be distinguished in life.

In any case, the spiral was/is very important to the *Eunano* and its relatives. It decorated the skulls of *Eunano*, the coins of the incipient *Leprechaun (Boyne River)*, the cremation Celtic Brick of the incipient *Gnome*, the belt buckle of the *Texas Gnome*, and the casket of the *Connolly Leprechaun*. It's interesting that the Iberian Celts (Beakers) carried the spiral to Ireland but it didn't last. Nor did the spiral catch on for the Celtic derived peoples of northern Europe.

I am tempted to assign significance to another design on the top of the *Eunano* skull. The temptation is to consider it a four leaf clover which would have that symbol of Ireland an import as well. But I fear that stretches probability a bit too far.

Since the *Duendes* of southern Mexico are the same size as the *Eunano* and since the word *Duende* is the only Spanish word the Indians of the region use (there's no Nahuatll word for *Duende*), I suspect some *Eunano* made it to America aboard Spanish sailing ships of the 15th and 16th Centuries to become the *Duendes*.

Figure 81 *Close-up of Nyami Nyami skull.*

Nyami Nyami

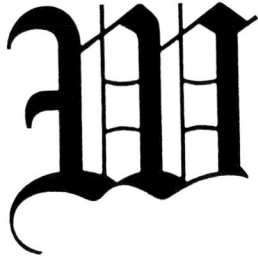

hen Dallasite, Elaine Ackley, returned from an international white water competition in Zimbabwe, south central Africa, during the fall of '95, she called to say that she had recovered a fossil *Nyami Nyami* from the banks of the Zambezi River. I had to admit that I had never heard of a *Nyami Nyami*. Elaine referred me to Professor Todd Brownell, THE expert on *Nyami Nyami*.

It seems that *Nyami Nyami* has the head of a crocodile and the body of a snake. Many years ago *Nyami Nyami* and his wife lived in an area around Kariba on the Zambezi River. One day, his wife went upstream through the Kariwa Gorge to answer the prayers and bless the people of the valley. While she was gone, white men came to build a wall (dam) across the river. *Nyami Nyami* was very unhappy and caused many floods and much loss of life. Finally, however, the elders of the Tonga tribe and their medium spirits persuaded him to allow the Zambezi to be tamed by the Kariba Lake. Even though *Nyami Nyami* is now separated from his wife, he has become a Guardian Spirit of those who travel the Zambezi, if they praise his spirit.

I should learn not to be surprised by what my friends find on their adventures, but I seem to always be skeptical until shown. "A hybrid between a crocodile and a snake, indeed!" My skepticism frustrated Elaine, who does know her wildlife, so she was as excited as I when the rock she had shipped arrived in Houston. We took my trailer to retrieve the crate from dock storage. Neither of us could wait until after the long drive back to Dallas, so we opened the crate right there in the parking lot.

Unless some very clever prankster had discovered a fossil crocodile skull and a skeleton of a large snake with the exact same preservation and then prepared the two together expertly, she did indeed have something I had never seen before. And, to be sure, it does have anatomical features of both snakes and crocs. Crocodiles and snakes are only related in the most distant way by both belonging to the class Reptilia, but then, when dealing with mythical creatures, I've learned that anything is possible.

We took the specimen to the University Preparation Laboratory and I scratched and etched some of the excess sediments from around the ribs and vertebrae, leaving nothing to the imagination. Most certainly this creature deserves its own name considering its uniqueness.

Nyaminyami ackleyi, new genus and species

Figs. 81, 83

Holotype: LU 65348 Complete skeleton still in matrix.

Diagnosis: Vertebrae most closely matching the features of a reticulated python; Skull resembles that of a typical crocodilian.

Etymology: *Nyaminyami*, the generic name given, is a Latinized version of the vernacular name for the creature + *ackleyi* in honor of the fossil's discoverer, Elaine Ackley.

Description: The story of *Nyami Nyami*

doesn't indicate its ophidean relationships beyond being part snake. The vertebrae are identical to those of the extant reticulated python but the skull contains all of the features of a typical crocodilian, *i.e.*, the secondary palate includes closed palatals and pterygoids.

Then, there is the matter of size— this specimen stretched to maximum length would be about five feet long. From the stories, one gets the impression that they grow somewhat larger, even though *Nyami Nyami* never show themselves in their entirety. It would seem that in spite of being mythical, *Nyami Nyami* are hatched, have a normal growing up period, and are subject to mortality under certain circumstances. This specimen is therefore considered an immature offspring of the River God, *Nyami Nyami*

Discovery: Elaine said that she and her crew had beached their raft to take a short rest when she strolled to the base of the cliff walling them in. There was a rubble pile of sandstone flags that had appeared to have fallen from high above. Apparently, the river had undercut the cliff, spalling off some of its surface including the face of a cave exposed about thirty feet up. The flags were probably part of the cave floor since the stone and its color was very different from the rock lens showing in the face of the cliff.

The flagstone containing the *Nyami Nyami* is apparently one section of a mosaic caused by mud cracking, due to the sediments being subjected to dry air after deposition. It is difficult to imagine such a river being completely dry long enough for mud cracks to form. Furthermore, the fine grained sediments of the flagstone certainly were not deposited in a raging river. Normally the cave pond would be replenished by flood waters even though it was some thirty feet above the normal stream. I believe that the creature, as well as the associated

Figure 82 *Nyami Nyami locality map.*

139

fish, found themselves in the cave pond at a time when the river did not rise the thirty feet needed to replenish the water, which accounts for the death of the *Nyami Nyami* and associated fish.

The flagstone containing the *Nyami Nyami* remains was far too heavy to carry aboard the raft, so Elaine inquired if the accompanying helicopter might take it out for her. It was a lot to ask, but Elaine is very persuasive and she accomplished what any lesser person could have never done, including yours truly.

Although the subject of *Nyami Nyami* came up several times during the journey, the others didn't seem to recognize the dual snake/croc features in Elaine's fossil. She didn't really talk about her suspicions beyond saying it was her very own *Nyami Nyami*, in a joking manner. . . . After all, *Nyami Nyami* are mythical, Right?

Figure 83 *Nyami Nyami skeleton*

Figure 83 *Nyami Nyami fossil skeleton.*

140

As a paleontologist, it's my bent to try to organize creatures into some sort of scheme so they (1) may be discussed properly, and (2) may be understood better. I have attempted to place these creatures in their proper place with respect to each other and humans. I've done this using the same tools as we use in more normal evolution studies, based on the evolution of selected parts (teeth, feet, horns, etc.). Recent DNA and protein studies have been shown to accurately reflect relationships between groups of animals, as well. For example, a human and a rabbit share more proteins than a human and a lizard. Humans and monkeys share less than humans and chimpanzees, and so on.

I submitted samples of bone to Dr. Gil King, Director of the King Forensic Laboratories, to map DNA proteins. I'm pleased to report that Dr. King's conclusions, using these modern techniques, match my own fairly closely. I therefore have prepared a sort of cladogram, or family tree, drawing on both techniques (Fig. 84). Examples are: Oni with three toes feet (perrisodactyl) is more closely related to the two toed or cloven hoofed forms (artiodactyl) such as *Pan* and *Kokopelli*, than to the carnivore-footed *Skadaria*. On the other hand, the cloven hoofed forms are more closely related to each other than either is to the three toed form. *Neptunoides* and *Kappa* seem distantly related to each other and even more distantly related to the *Mermaids*. *Leprechauns* and *Gnomes*, with no basic differences in their skeletons and those of modern humans, are closest to humanity in protein make-up as well. *Rugaru* is a little more distant, but still very close. The flying Isusu and the fairies are about as distantly related to humans as the mermaids.

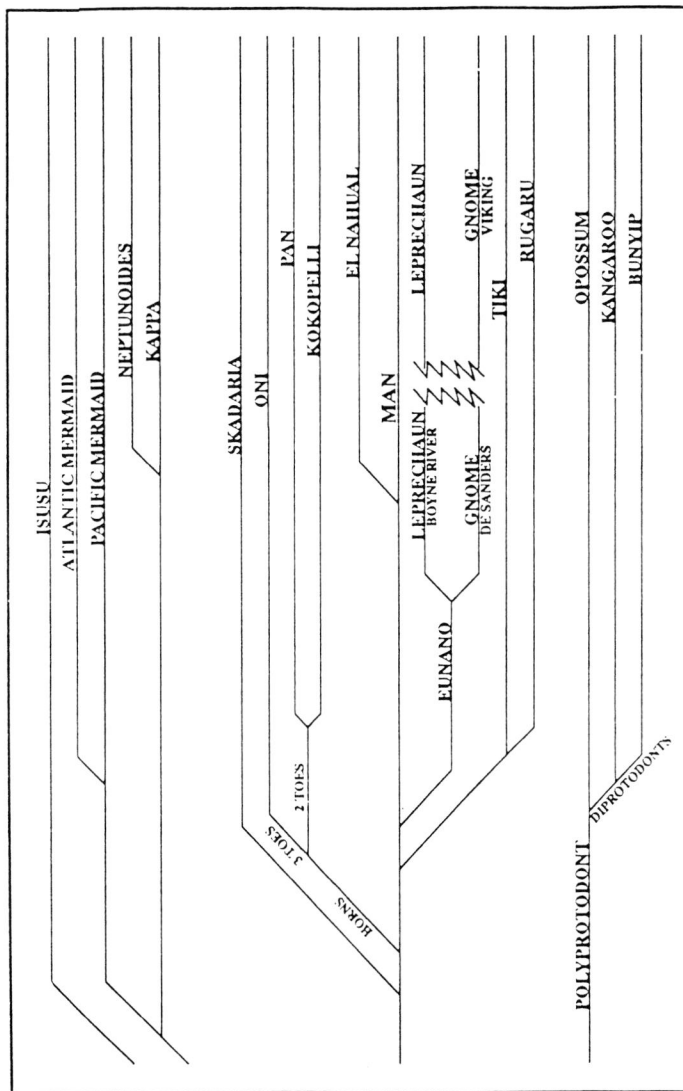

Figure 84 *Tree showing suggested relationships.*

LONGEVITY

It has recently been shown that the age of a person at death can be estimated fairly accurately by studying a section of bone. Bone is constantly being remodeled, leaving behind osteons in the form of tubes through the bone. These tubes slowly fill with new bone precipitated on on their walls. The more osteons are in a given area, the more the bone has been remodeled and therefore the older the individual was. The more the number of re-modeling tubes (osteons), the smaller percent of the mass is made up of the original lamellar bone. Shows the relationship between osteon density, lamellar bone, and age. Based on the charts developed to age human bones, Neptunoides would be in excess of two hundred years old (Fig. 85). Furthermore, since the bone is totally remodeled, it could have been remodeled many times and the age could be many times that estimate. We found that the bones of all of these creatures except for the *Leprechauns*, *Gnomes*, *Rugaru*, and *El Nahual* and *Windigo* are like *Neptunoides*. The *Leprechauns* and *Gnomes* are like man suggesting similar periods of longevity. *Rugaru*, although very man-like in his DNA sequences, would be less than fifteen years old by the charts. This is clearly in error since the epiphysis of his bones are fused, indicating he is adult. Even more amazing is the bone of the *Windigo*. It is made of e ntirely lamellar bone which would indicate he was newborn! We must admit that there is some other method of

bone growth involved than we are familiar with.

All this tells us that there is some organized evolution in the background of these beings similar to, but separate from, that of humans. It also suggests that certain types like *Leprechauns*, and *Gnomes* are not so very old as groups and could have branched from the human lineage directly.

I conclude these stories as I began them—

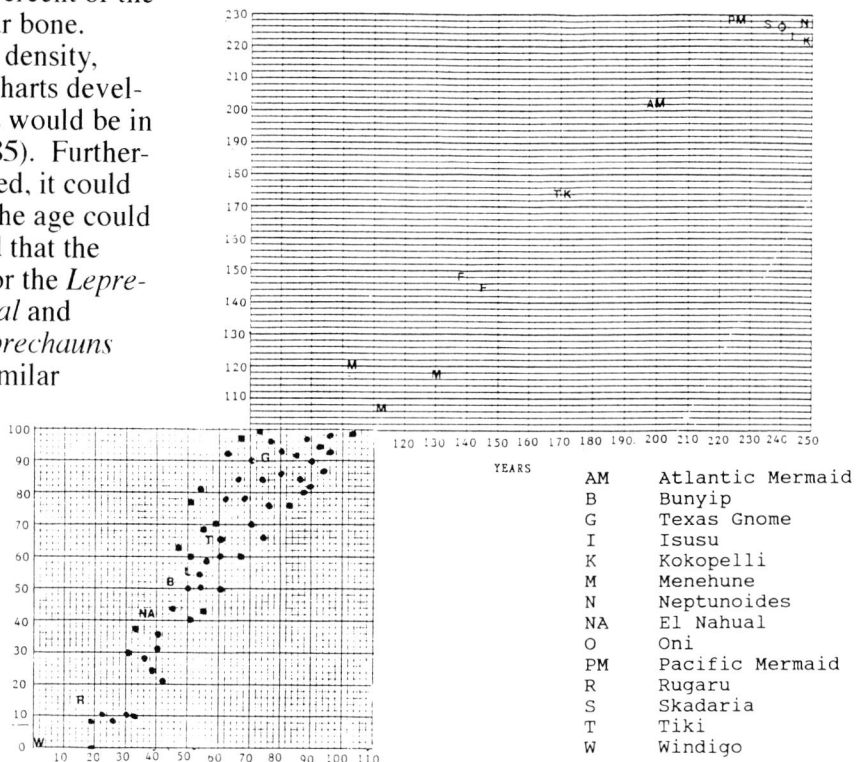

Figure 85 *Scatter diagram showing probable longevity based on osteon density.*

AM	Atlantic Mermaid
B	Bunyip
G	Texas Gnome
I	Isusu
K	Kokopelli
M	Menehune
N	Neptunoides
NA	El Nahual
O	Oni
PM	Pacific Mermaid
R	Rugaru
S	Skadaria
T	Tiki
W	Windigo

142

CONCLUSIONS

intrigued, confused, and without profound answers to the huge questions that remain, not the least of which is the disparity of the fossil record and the shortage of time required for such creatures to evolve. Combinations of human and animal features such as those presented in mermaids, fairies and hoofed homonoids would clearly take tens of millions of years to evolve in the proven fashion, if indeed they ever could. And since man himself has only a couple of million years tenure, something else is in play.

I've already mentioned the possibility of there being a sort of other dimension in which these beings evolved under different rules, but from which they occasionally venture into our dimension. Even if this is so, the rate of evolution would have to be much greater or there would have to be considerably more time available.

Another sobering thought is that these creatures probably do not, and have not, existed outside of human minds at all. The human mind is an amazing and, we think, unique organ capable of creating almost anything he/she wants. As Mircea Eliade pointed out, until a few decades ago western scholars thought of myth as fables, fiction, invention, etc. In these more enlightened times, ethnologists, socialogists, anthropologists, historians of religion, and others interested in myth, acknowledge that in many societies myth means "true story."

Myth tells a sacred history, relating events that took place in Primordial Time, near the Beginning. It describes how reality came into existence and therefore gives accounts of creation through the activities of Supernatural Beings. A myth might relate the creation of the cosmos, of the shell of the turtle, of the seasons, but almost always creation. Archaic societies point to the reality of the world as proof of the myth (account) of its origin. A common thread through most religions is that man was first immortal but displeased God and became mortal. No one doubts that man dies so this testifies to man's fall from grace.

People who study evolution, like myself, often accomodate Genesis by pointing out that a week in Primordial Time doesn't necessaryly equate with seven days as we know them. All religions (indeed, all cosmologies) studied in detail begin with a period of Primordial Time when todays rules were not in effect. The creation of each reality is a part of myth and a result of the activities of Supernatural Beings, or creatures. Culture is an evolutionary process, like natural selection. Each succeeding culture begins where its predescessor left off. Myths and mythical creatures serve as exemplary models for human behavior and values. If these behaviors and values are beneficial to culture, they will remain after the myth has been forgotten and the starring Supernatural Being's name has ceased to be uttered. They affect concepts and ideas and thereby live on. Herein may lie the answer to your questions. The creatures described here are real, like the world. You can see and touch them. If its the origin of their persona that you seek, study their myths. If its the origin of their remains that you seek, you must first understand the motives and primordial thoughts of their creators. Good luck.